Corporate Governance
for the Irish Arts Sector

Corporate Governance for the Irish Arts Sector

Penelope Kenny

Chartered
Accountants
Ireland

Published in 2014 by
Chartered Accountants Ireland
Chartered Accountants House
47–49 Pearse Street
Dublin 2
www.charteredaccountants.ie

ISBN 978-1-908199-28-7

Typeset by Datapage
Printed by CPI Group (UK) Ltd, Croydon, CR0 4YY

For Richard, Dearbhaile, Donal, David, Eamonn, Deirde and Fiona.

Contents

Foreword

The arts, we are told by authoritative sources as varied as Hegel and Geoffrey Hartman, can variously be described as 'sacred', the 'visible appearance of God's Kingdom on earth', 'breathing spiritual dispositions into us', and inspiring love in the highest part of the soul. They have a "higher reality and more veritable existence" (Hegel) than ordinary life and express the eternal and reveal the "innermost nature of the world" (Schopenhauer). There may be many who feel that these descriptions are too connected to a deity, but there is general agreement that the arts form a separate and important part of our lives and that they should be kept apart from the contaminants of money and sex.

However, over many centuries, the role of the patrons of the arts, in providing money, has been undeniable, from ancient Rome to Medieval and Renaissance Europe up to the present time. Of course, patronage of the arts was not always appreciated: Samuel Johnson described the patron of the arts as "one who looks with unconcern on a man struggling for life in the water, and, when he has reached ground, encumbers him with help". It is, however, doubtful whether we would now have such a rich artistic treasure store were it not for the patron – the funder, both individual and corporate.

This book recognises the current important role the funder of the arts has in our society and the concomitant need to provide assurance that the funds provided have been disposed of in accordance with the objectives outlined in the application for funding. This requires a high level of corporate governance.

This book provides a valuable reference for financial advisors to arts organisations and to the members of the boards of those organisations, many of whom may be generously endowed with artistic gifts, but not with an expert understanding of the current societal demand for good corporate governance. It is also a useful and interesting source of information about the background to governance in the arts sector, and a must-have handbook for directors, auditors, financial advisors, the Arts Council and donors involved in or with the arts.

Professor Patricia Barker
November 2014

Preface

As an accountant and student of cultural policy, I am convinced that accountants can learn diversity and creativity from the arts sector, and that the arts sector can learn transparency and accountability from accountants. This book is written from my experiences, work and studies on governance in the arts sector – research for which I am grateful to my clients and friends.

I am privileged to work with arts organisations and funders of arts organisations. It is a wonderfully rich sector that contributes hugely to communities and society. It is a sector that governments and funders continue to nurture and protect, despite the hard times.

Despite the significant strategic benefits of corporate governance for arts organisations, governance is still mainly driven by the funders and grant-givers. Furthermore, governance within arts organisations can be treated as an isolated topic, grouped with the organisations' financial accounting; many small arts organisations expect their auditors or accountants to "take care of all that". There is little evidence of alignment of governance with organisational aims and objectives. In an environment where organisational effectiveness is paramount to achieving value for stakeholders, most arts organisations are not leveraging corporate governance to achieve greater effectiveness.

Current changes in legislation, budgetary cutbacks and changes in public opinion are causing arts organisations to review how they are funded and to emphasise the visibility of their corporate governance practices. Arts organisations, and those who fund them, are increasingly emphasising good corporate governance as a prerequisite for funding. This book highlights the many positive aspects of governance in evidence in the sector already, while highlighting how well-governed organisations are more likely to obtain, and maintain, funding and public support.

The guiding principle behind this book is that good governance is an indicator of successful arts organisations, and that without alignment of governance and artistic aims, artistic merit can be lost. This book identifies best practices in the arts and business sectors of accounting and governance, and how to use them to mutual benefit. Throughout this book, practices and definitions from both the financial and accounting sectors and the arts and cultural sectors are explored to develop a best practice framework and to show that the basic principles of corporate governance are the same for all organisations.

People working in arts organisations are increasingly aware that good corporate governance is a prerequisite to seeking funding from external sources, and that it must be a cornerstone of their income-generating strategies. Governance standards are set out in the Irish Companies Act and by best practices used in Ireland (e.g. from the *UK Corporate Governance Code*); these standards are applied to all corporate entities. Arts organisations are mainly based in the non-profit sector; they are often companies limited by guarantee, sometimes with charitable status, sometimes without; and sometimes they hold valuable assets such as buildings and venues. Their success is often largely defined by the affirmation of their values rather than the achievement of profits, and their artistic programmes usually stretch their budgets to the last penny. If they have a surplus, it is often to fund medium or long-term programmes.

My studies in this area have been fruitful and enjoyable. A few years ago, I was required to write a thesis as part of a master's degree in Cultural Policy and Arts Management in University College Dublin (UCD). I was convinced that my thesis would almost write itself (this was disproven!). I wrote from the perspective of an accountant contributing to the arts sector, hence the title: *Corporate Governance for the Irish Arts Sector*. For UCD, this was the first thesis on corporate governance on the Cultural Policy and Arts Management course. The contributions of Pat Cooke and Dr Emily Mark-Fitzgerald of that department were huge. The Institute of Chartered Accountants readily introduced me to chartered accountants working and volunteering in the Irish arts sector. There were quite a few; all of them had a great appreciation for what the cultural sector brings to our society and to our business thinking. They were also unanimous that corporate governance is not high up on the agenda for our arts organisations, not least for financial reasons. It was clear that those organisations would benefit greatly from a book or publication for their own sector, from within the sector.

This book is therefore a response to the importance of the arts and cultural sector and the increased demands for visibility and transparency in the operation of it. Its intended users are managers, directors, officers, accountants and auditors of arts organisations, including theatre, music, the visual arts and organisations who represent arts organisations. It refers to recent legislative initiatives with guidelines, codes and websites, together with recommendations on how best to use the body of information to align strategy, operations and management and demonstrate accountability, transparency and stewardship. The detailed chapter contents, together with the bibliography and appendices, are designed to help readers to use this book as a reference tool.

Above all, this book is designed to be readable and comprehensively referenced to help the reader. I hope you enjoy it.

Introduction

Corporate governance is the system by which organisations are directed and controlled. In the arts sector, corporate governance is currently the subject of significant public interest and debate. There are two main reasons for this public interest. First, the recession that struck in 2008 is believed to have been aggravated by a series of systemic business failures. These failures have led to heightened awareness about the adequacy of the systems of corporate governance used by all of our institutions, not least our arts organisations. Moreover, some high-profile instances of corporate governance failures have occurred in the arts sector. Negative publicity in relation to misappropriation of funds and the appropriateness of payments to directors have received significant media coverage, indicating the sensitivity of the community to financial scandals in our funded organisations. Secondly, the landscape of funding is changing: government funding is being reduced for all sectors, and the arts sector is no exception. Arts organisations are identifying the need to look for funding from a variety of sources. These organisations must therefore be fundable. This means being transparent, accountable and having proper controls in place to safeguard the funds. Essentially, these organisations must be able to demonstrate good corporate governance.

In the current market environment, increased corporate governance is essential to protecting the long-term success of the sector. The 2009 publication of the *Code of Practice for the Governance of State Bodies* by the Department of Finance and the establishment of the Charities Regulatory Authority for the non-profit sector (announced in July 2013) are examples of the heightened awareness in Ireland of the need for better regulation and better governance in the sector. Governance standards, and awareness of those standards, are slowly evolving in the sector.

The Charities Act 2009 was enacted as a result of strong lobbying for governance from within and outside of the non-profit sector (a large part of the arts sector can be considered as a subset of the non-profit sector). Prior to its enactment, the sector proliferated with debate, governance guides and recommendations, which contributed to the drafting of the Charities

Act legislation. It is important to note, however, that the Irish Charities Act has been enacted but its implementation was halted in 2011, and is now being restarted on a more cost-conscious basis. The sector is preparing for the full implementation of new legislation through discussion, debate and recommendations.

Alongside the planning, drafting and enactment of the Charities Act 2009, a number of infrastructural organisations have been established in the sector. The Governance Code for Community, Voluntary and Charitable Organisations was launched in June 2012 by eight non-profit organisations. This code of governance is described as having been developed "for the sector by the sector". The code has become more important since the delay in implementing the Charities Act, and it is being widely adopted.

It is against this background that this book investigates how governance is applied, what frameworks are used to implement it, and how funders can imbue their funded arts organisations with good governance. Most importantly, this book shows how the best practices in corporate governance can be utilised to realise organisational objectives. It also uses experiences and anecdotes from my own consultancy practice in the area of governance of arts and cultural organisations in both the non-profit and for-profit sectors.

The study that preceded this book enquired into the links between good governance of our cultural institutions, specifically our arts organisations, and the giving of grants and funds to the cultural sector in Ireland. At a time when Irish cultural institutions are braced for ongoing and significant grant cuts, fundraising from various sources (other than the Arts Council) may well be the only way for those institutions to maintain their status. If this becomes the case, Irish arts organisations may need to become better prepared to apply for and to receive funds from other private and philanthropic sources. These sources of funding will be new for many arts and cultural organisations, and those organisations will need to prove their good governance to both traditional and new funders and funding sources. They may require more visible governance structures, including more transparency and financial accountability, which is outlined in this book.

There are some governance issues which are common to organisations in many sectors and others that are peculiar to the arts sector. This book offers up-to-date information for the arts sector, referring to all of the recent legislative initiatives with guidelines, codes and websites. It includes recommendations on how to best use the body of information to align strategy, operations and management. As part of the study which preceded this book, it was discovered that there were few definitive publications for arts organisations and their advisors that could provide a comprehensive framework within which arts organisations can implement, measure and judge their own corporate governance frameworks. This book tries to fill that gap, and hopefully other publications will follow.

Acknowledgements

The acknowledgement of those who helped, advised and collaborated to produce this book is a very important section. The people who were asked for help or were interviewed were identified as stakeholders of corporate governance in the arts sector. They are acknowledged here, with recognition that this book is made possible only with the collaboration of the accountancy and the arts sectors. This recognition helps define the valuable collaborative space and serves to highlight the potential for further sharing of interests by both sectors.

I would like to acknowledge the good advice of my friends and colleagues in University College Dublin, Professor Niamh Brennan, and, in the Department of Art History, Pat Cooke, Dr Emily Mark-Fitzgerald and Elizabeth Varley; my friends and colleagues from Chartered Accountants Ireland, Professor Patricia Barker and Daisy Downes; from the Ireland Funds, Jordan Campbell, David Duffy, Caitriona Fotterell, Tom O'Leary, Marjorie Muldowney and Bart Murphy; from the San Francisco Ballet, Tom Flynn and Kim Ondreck Carim and Irial O'Farrell, whose experiences of publishing her own book have been invaluable for me; from the Arts Council, Karin McCully and Judith Woodworth; also my family, friends and neighbours, Sally Ann Flood, Vivienne Jupp, Michael Kenny, Jennifer Kenny, David Kenny, Caroline Bergin and the late Dr Rosemarie Mulcahy, all of whose generosity of spirit, intelligence and insights lit the way for this study and shone a light on what excellence might look like.

The kind direction and keen interest and encouragement from individual Arts Council staff, Orlaith McBride, Director; Michelle Hoctor, Communications Director; Martin O'Sullivan, Finance Director; and Val Ballance, Head of Venues, has been a driving force for identifying the various aspects of corporate governance in Ireland's wide and varied arts sector.

My sincere thanks also for the insights and generous advice, direction and wisdom from Ray Yeates, Dublin City Arts Officer. Also to Andrew Hetherington, Business to Arts; Tina Roche, CEO, Business in the Community Ireland; Deirdre Garvey, CEO, The Wheel; Jane Daly and Siobhan Bourke from the Irish Theatre Institute; and my friend and fellow student Anna Walsh, Director of Theatre Forum Ireland.

Finally, my thanks to Michael Diviney, Director of Publishing, Chartered Accountants Ireland, Dan Bolger and Lisa Coen. Their encouragement, professional advice and constructive editing helped to make what I hope is now a cohesive, useful and readable book.

Chapter 1

Defining Arts and Governance: Why is Good Governance so Important?

Corporate governance is more than regulatory compliance, it is about the alignment of strategy, operations and management; it is also about accountability, transparency and stewardship.
Financial Reporting Council (2010)

Introduction

For all arts organisations, producing or enabling good art is the primary goal and measure of success, and certainly this should never change. Attempts to quantify output or to identify value for money indicators are of limited benefit and burdensome to many arts organisations (as argued in **Chapter 6**). What is important, however, is that arts organisations in receipt of public monies can justify their expenditures and show some transparency and accountability. This will also be useful for those organisations when they are seeking further funding. It is vital for the arts sector as a whole that it can show that it is well run with minimum financial mistakes or scandals. We have seen the withdrawal of public trust and confidence in the entire Irish banking sector in recent years; the arts sector, despite recent negative publicity, is by comparison more trusted, deemed more suitable for state funding and is seen to be serving the public's needs.

To discuss the arts sector it is necessary first to define it. The definition must be a general one, however, because as is typical of a creative and constantly innovating sector, arts organisations continuously regroup and evolve. The sector is composed of organisations housed in large permanent buildings, such as the national galleries, and also of much smaller and transient organisations, such as theatre production companies that might receive a once-off grant and disband when the money is spent.

Practical observations of governance in the sector show that it is made up of well-meaning and diligent people driven by a passion to produce art. Corporate governance issues often arise from lack of knowledge or hands-on expertise, or lack of resources. They sometimes arise from lack of controls, checks and balances, and this can leave the organisation exposed to loss or misappropriation that would not have occurred if simple control features were in place. While the adoption of good governance principles can provide structure and stability, and a diligent board of directors will go a long way to redress these gaps, as will be shown in **Chapters 4** and **5**, boards can also lack effectiveness due to their composition, the appointment process or even their organisation. The adoption of good governance principles can work to provide structure and stability.

What is the 'Arts Sector'?

My experience in the sector varies from work with large grant-givers to small, one-person organisations; from permanent collections and programmes to once-off festivals and events. The fact is that the arts sector in Ireland is large and economically significant. It is a huge employer and receives significant funding from public and private sources. However, what is meant by the 'arts sector' varies. This book employs the Arts Council of Ireland's definition, and focuses on organisations producing creative output and receiving grants to do so. The sector is composed of diverse organisations producing recognised art forms. The Arts Council-recognised art forms are: "architecture, circus, dance, film, literature, music, opera, street arts and spectacle, theatre, traditional arts and visual arts".[1]

The arts sector is also associated and grouped with the non-profit sector in Ireland. The non-profit sector is loosely defined as having charitable tax status and many arts organisations operate as non-profits. The income for these organisations in Ireland was estimated at €838 million in 2004.[2] The Irish arts sector is a subset of the cultural, charity and the non-profit sectors, so many of the reports and guides referring to the characteristics of these wider sectors are relevant to the arts sector and arts organisations.

In his book *Economics and Culture*, the academic David Throsby defines the creative arts as: "music, dance, theatre, literature, the visual arts, the crafts, and including newer forms of practice such as video art, performance art, computer and multimedia art and so on."[3] He further defines the arts industry as follows:

[1] These definitions are found on the Arts Council website (www.artscouncil.ie).
[2] Donoghue, F., O'Regan, A., McGee, S. and Donovan, A.M., "Exploring the Irish Fundraising Landscape: A report on the practice and scale of charitable fundraising from the Republic of Ireland" (2007), Irish Charities Tax Research Limited, Centre for Nonprofit Management, School of Business, Trinity College Dublin.
[3] Throsby, D., *Economics and Culture* (Cambridge University Press, 2001).

"An aggregation of all the art forms within a region, a nation, etc., together with their attendant service providers, can be seen to comprise the arts industry as a whole for that region, nation or whatever other unit is the focus of the study."[4]

However, it is difficult to sharply define what we mean by the 'arts sector', as the boundaries of the sector are blurred. Nevertheless, the definition of an **arts organisation** that this book will use is **an organisation receiving some form of grant aid, or outside assistance from the community, in order to facilitate creative output**. This will allow us to focus on the need for corporate governance in environments where effective, visible and demonstrable corporate governance can lead to more funding, as greater funding would lead arts organisations to further their creative vision and goals.

Broadly speaking, the arts sector in Ireland is made up of a number of different types of organisation. Some organisations may even belong to two or more of these categories:

- Non-profit companies limited by guarantee.
- Organisations with charitable status.
- Private limited companies.
- State-owned or State-controlled bodies.
- Unincorporated organisations who may act as sole traders.

For example, many arts organisations are companies limited by guarantee with charitable status. Some State-controlled bodies are private limited companies; some unincorporated entities may have charitable status. Other arts organisations form on the receipt of a grant, and disband when the grant money is spent and the project is complete. Clearly, the legal structures are not straightforward to categorise.

Size of the Irish Arts Sector

There is a need for a more comprehensive, more fine-tuned quantification of the arts sector in Ireland. Quantifying the arts sector will allow policy-makers to identify grant needs, employment opportunities and likely cultural and social impacts. It will also help those involved in corporate governance to categorise the sector in terms of the needs of an effective corporate governance programme.

---

[4] *Ibid.*

According to a report by Indecon, commissioned by the Arts Council and published in 2012, the total 'gross value-added'[5] for arts organisations in Ireland in 2011 was estimated at €713.25 million. The same report defines the wider arts sector as: "Arts Council funding recipients; film and video; literature and publishing; library, archives, museums and other cultural activities; operation of arts facilities; and artistic and literacy creation and interpretation". This wider arts sector directly employed 12,972 full-time people in 2011; when direct, indirect and induced employment are aggregated, the figure is 20,755 full-time employees.[6]

Further quantification of the sector was carried out by the Irish Nonprofits Knowledge Exchange ('INKEx'). In its 2012 report, "Irish Nonprofits: What do we know?",[7] which describes itself as "the first-ever report to provide access to rich data from a full, extensive population of Irish nonprofits", INKEx identified 650 organisations in Ireland as belonging to the arts sector. Only organisations registered with the Companies Registration Office (CRO) are included in the survey, therefore all unincorporated entities are excluded. INKEx calculated that "of the 1,963 nonprofits concerned with culture or recreation, about 650 are culture, arts or heritage organisations".[8]

This figure may be conservative, judging by older research from 2006. The work of the Centre for Nonprofit Management at Trinity College has helped identify the size of the non-profit sector in Ireland, and within that research some figures are available for the arts sector. The Centre estimated that there were between 350 and 1,477 arts organisations in Ireland in 2006,[9] some funded by the Arts Council, others unfunded; some of these

---

[5] The Arts Council, "Assessment of Economic Impact of the Arts in Ireland: An Update Report" (November 2012), Arts and Culture Scoping Research Project by Indecon International Economic Consultants. 'Gross value-added' (GVA) is defined as the difference between the value of goods and services produced for any given sector and the cost of intermediate inputs and consumption used in the production process. It is the nearest equivalent at the sector level to gross domestic product (GDP), when measured across the economy as a whole.

[6] *Ibid.* Indecon defines 'induced' as arising from the multiplier effect.

[7] Irish Nonprofits Knowledge Exchange, "Irish Nonprofits: What do we know?" (January 2012).

[8] *Ibid.*

[9] Donoghue, F., O'Regan, A., McGee, S. and Donovan, A.M., "Exploring the Irish Fundraising Landscape: A report on the practice and scale of charitable fundraising from the Republic of Ireland" (2007), Irish Charities Tax Research Limited, Centre for Nonprofit Management, School of Business, Trinity College Dublin.

are incorporated entities and others are sole traders or otherwise unincorporated.[10]

In terms of organisational size, the average arts organisation in Ireland is often very small. A survey carried out by Business to Arts and Deloitte in 2008 showed that "55% of participating arts organisations have less than five employees".[11] Scale is an important factor in determining the scope of corporate governance programmes in organisations, as smaller organisations will have simpler governance programmes than larger ones. The small size of typical arts organisations can dictate the resources and expertise available for corporate governance activities.

Organisational Size and Corporate Governance

The *Governance Code for Community, Voluntary and Charitable Organisations in Ireland* (for the purposes of this book, 'the Governance Code') states: "The way that governance is exercised will vary from one organisation to the next depending on a number of factors such as size, level of funding and skills".[12] The Governance Code recognises the small size of many organisations in the non-profit sector, and the Code discusses a "proportionate approach", defining three categories of organisation (A, B and C), described below and based on how governance is conducted. These categories are defined by governance roles for the board. The role of the board for category A organisations is "comprehensive, including governance, management and operations"; for category B, it is "primarily governance but with some management and operational responsibilities as well"; and for category C, it is "solely governance, with a clear division between the governance role of the board and the management and operations role of staff".[13] The distinctions between these categories are left to the organisations to decide, as the code is voluntary.

Identifying the size and distinctions of arts organisations can help provide tailored guidelines for the sector. Although the sector and its boundaries may be difficult to define, good corporate governance can still be readily defined and identified. What good governance means can vary from application

---

[10] *Ibid.*

[11] Business to Arts, "Private Investment in Arts and Culture: Survey Report" (Deloitte, 2008).

[12] The *Governance Code for Community, Voluntary and Charitable Organisations in Ireland* (2011), www.governancecode.ie.

[13] *Ibid.*

to application, but it is always founded on the principles of leadership, effectiveness and accountability.

As with every organisational initiative, basic considerations of costs and benefits apply. In the financial sector, Ireland has recently seen the result of light-touch regulation and low governance standards, which have cost many billions of euro. Ultimately, the benefits of good corporate governance outweigh its costs. It is true that amongst many small arts organisations the proportionate costs of governance programmes can become significant. This has been largely taken into account, however, for example, section 50 of the Charities Act 2009 recognises that 'one size fits all' legislation can penalise smaller entities, and the Act therefore grants smaller organisations an exemption from the audit requirement. The Irish non-profit sector's voluntary governance code, the *Governance Code for Community, Voluntary and Charitable Organisations*, recognises that: "These organisations cannot be expected to devote limited resources to the development and support of sophisticated governance systems."[14] However, the Governance Code states that governance principles[15] remain constant "no matter the size or stage of development of an organisation".[16]

Good corporate governance in Irish arts organisations should help define shared measures of success, and how they are formed and agreed upon between the organisation and its stakeholders. There has been considerable discussion about the synchronicities and dynamics between donors and donees and grant-givers and receivers, as well as the appropriateness of the relationship between the two parties. For example, an arts organisation serving the public cannot take grants from organisations which do not serve the public interest or are engaged in illegal activities. Good governance sets strategy and enables organisations to seek appropriate funding sources with an agreement of the objectives and outcomes for both parties. This is a dynamic relationship designed to benefit both parties.

In a discussion of competing demands, the working paper "The Many Faces of Nonprofit Accountability", by Alnoor Ebrahim, asks: "…is it feasible, or even desirable, for nonprofit organizations to be accountable to

---

[14] The Governance Code (2011), www.governancecode.ie.
[15] The Governance Code defines the five principles as: 1. Providing leadership; 2. Exercising control; 3. Being transparent and accountable; 4. Working effectively; 5. Behaving with integrity.
[16] The Governance Code (2011), www.governancecode.ie.

everyone for everything?"[17] It can be argued that arts organisations are not very different from all other organisations in this respect: many organisations complain about the costs of legislative and best-practice compliance while simultaneously running their businesses. Ebrahim highlights this by declaring simply that: "The challenge for leadership and management is to prioritize among competing accountability demands."[18] We will now discuss this prioritisation in the context of the Irish arts sector in Ireland.

The Main Funders of the Irish Arts Sector

Although many arts organisations are successful at earning money and the sector is financially significant, core capital and operational funding tend to come from outside the sector. This is important, because whereas the responsibility for corporate governance lies with the arts organisations, the public funders have the power to drive and improve governance standards in the sector (a dynamic that is discussed further in **Chapter 2**). Therefore, identifying the main public funders and their needs and goals is also relevant.

Despite the current emphasis on seeking funds from more diverse sources, the Arts Council continues to be the largest funder by far of the arts in Ireland. In 2012 it gave grants of €56.6 million (down from €58 million in 2011).[19] The disproportionate size of their funding suggests that the Arts Council is likely to remain the largest funder of most arts organisations for the foreseeable future.

By comparison, Dublin City Council's arts funding for 2014 was budgeted at €530,000.[20] For 2012, the Ireland Funds, which is privately funded, gave grants in Ireland of €2 million (in 2011 it gave €0.75 million), but only a small portion of these grants were given to the arts sector.[21] (The stated mission of the Ireland Funds is to support "peace and reconciliation, arts and culture, education and community development throughout the island of Ireland", and therefore their total funding must be shared amongst these sectors.[22])

---

[17] Ebrahim, A., "The Many Faces of Nonprofit Accountability (Working Paper No. 10-069)" (2010), Harvard Business School.
[18] *Ibid.*
[19] Arts Council Financial Statements for years ended 2011 and 2012.
[20] Arts Grants 2014 Recommendations, Dublin City Council Arts Office, Council Report REF: 2/2014, 3 January 2014.
[21] The American Ireland Funds Form 990, for 2011, submitted to the American Internal Revenue Service.
[22] www.theirelandfunds.org.

What is 'Corporate Governance'?

Corporate governance is a system of direction and control and this book discusses how to implement that system in arts organisations. The principles of good governance are leadership, effectiveness and accountability and transparency, and together these characteristics are generally accepted as the cornerstone of a good governance programme. The basic premise is that fundamental corporate governance principles exist for all organisations, regardless of their size. Therefore, the basic principles are the same for arts organisations as for large, profit-making corporations.

Governance comes from the board, and in many organisations a well-functioning board will be evident in efficient operations, evidence of vision, and clear direction and strategy. This is particularly true for arts organisations, where vision and strategy are the drivers of the artistic agenda and the organisational values come from the board. For arts organisations both large and small, this study contends that funders drive and request good governance standards. Furthermore, those organisations that display good governance will be easier to fund, and thus get more funds. Since governance is driven by the board, the board members are enablers for funding. This is discussed in greater detail below.

I have seen bad governance as the most common reason for funding cuts and for funds not being increased.

Corporate Governance and the Regulatory Framework

The 'regulatory framework' of a sector is the generally recognised laws, codes and best-practice guidelines that are in use, or can reasonably be expected to be used, in that sector. While 'framework' may be a very general concept, the structure of the regulatory framework can be easily identified.

First, all incorporated entities must comply with the Companies Acts, compliance with which is enforced by the Office of the Director of Corporate Enforcement (ODCE). Secondly, we can look to best practice in the UK, as "corporate governance policy in Ireland has followed the development of UK best practice".[23] Accounting practices and the legal structures of corporate entities are similar in the Irish and UK jurisdictions. For example, the ODCE also defines corporate governance as "the system by which companies are

[23] Hamill *et al.* (2010).

directed and controlled".[24] This definition applies to all types of entity, regardless of size and purpose. This definition comes from Financial Reporting Council's *Combined Code* of 2008, the precursor to the current *UK Corporate Governance Code*.[25] The ODCE uses and cites the *Combined Code* as best practice for Irish incorporated entities, and some of the guidance from the *Combined Code* is included in the Irish Companies (Auditing and Accounting) Act 2003.[26]

In 2009 the Irish Department of Finance issued an updated *Code of Practice for the Governance of State Bodies* ('the Code of Practice'); this Code of Practice defines corporate governance as "comprising the systems and procedures by which enterprises are directed and managed".[27] This definition is not dissimilar to that used by the ODCE. The Code of Practice states that it "provides a framework for the application of best practice in corporate governance by both commercial and non-commercial State bodies". These definitions are therefore being used by public sector funders and by large corporate funders – the two main funders of arts organisations. It is therefore appropriate that these definitions form the regulatory framework for the identification of corporate governance and its practices in the Irish arts sector.

The Alignment of Strategy, Operations and Management

According to the UK Corporate Governance Code: "Corporate governance is more than regulatory compliance, it is about the alignment of strategy, operations and management; it is also about accountability, transparency and stewardship."[28] Will well-governed arts organisations also achieve their artistic objectives? While no clear causal links have been established,[29] it is proposed that good governance is an enabling factor in arts organisations achieving their artistic objectives. Many funders of arts organisations in Ireland look for evidence of a well-run

---

[24] As defined in *The Report of the Committee on the Financial Aspects of Corporate Governance* (1992) ('The Cadbury Report'), see www.odce.ie.

[25] Financial Reporting Council, *The Combined Code* (2008).

[26] This book will therefore use definitions and guidance from the *Combined Code* and its updated version, the *UK Corporate Governance Code* (2012), issued by the Financial Reporting Council (FRC).

[27] Department of Finance, *Code of Practice for the Governance of State Bodies* (2009).

[28] Financial Reporting Council, *The UK Corporate Governance Code* (2010).

[29] In **Chapter 8** we examine the efforts of Johanne Turbide to identify a link between good governance and the operations of arts organisations. See Turbide, J., "Can Good Governance Prevent Financial Crises in Arts Organizations?" (2012) Vol. 14, No. 2, *International Journal of Arts Management*, 4–16.

organisation as a prerequisite for funding and grant-giving (see **Appendix 8** for examples of the information required by grant-givers prior to grant approvals).

Funders are aware that grant monies can be wasted by badly governed organisations. Most funders require that the organisation or entity be incorporated, with a board of directors, as reassurance that at least some governance structures are in place. For larger grant amounts, full due diligence is often carried out.[30] Therefore, it is reasonable to assert that arts organisations need to show some evidence of being well-governed in order to receive funding.

The monitoring of the governance of funded institutions by the funding bodies has become more critical as demands for better public accountability have increased. The existence of new sources of funding, for example the Creative Europe Programme 2014–2020 (with total funding of €1.8 billion, of which arts and culture will get €500 million[31]) has led to new conditions for awarding and monitoring grants, including guarantees and due diligence. Established funding bodies like the Arts Council are committed to general principles of good governance. The Arts Council emphasises "processes and practices in the allocation of public funds that demonstrate integrity, accountability, transparency and value for money".[32]

Benefits of a Good Governance Framework

Good governance can lead to more funding because it creates transparency and accountability. At a time when arts organisations are anticipating more grant cuts, it is important for them to optimise their ability to attract funding. The research behind this book included surveys of funders of arts organisations and their criteria for funding. In all cases, the funder was less concerned with artistic output (as this was a prerequisite for application) than they were that their funding would be well spent and used for the purpose for which it was given, in a fully transparent way.

Arts organisations are clear that governance must not hinder their artistic output, and I have observed good governance being an enabler of that output.

---

[30] For example, Atlantic Philanthropies carry out due diligence prior to giving large grants. This involves a full check and review of the financial well-being of the company, and its likely future well-being.

[31] http://ec.europa.eu/programmes/creative-europe (accessed 6 May 2013).

[32] The Arts Council, "Assessment of the Economic Impact of the Arts in Ireland" (November 2011), Arts and Culture Scoping Research Project by Indecon International Economic Consultants.

Interestingly, the research also shows that endorsement of good governance from the arts sector always comes with the caveat that corporate governance must never be a 'dead hand' or restrict innovation and creativity. The artists and arts managers interviewed were clear that, while they want good governance as an enabler for a well-run organisation that can access funding with relative ease, the dynamic balance of great art and good corporate governance must always fall on the side of great art. None of the guidelines or principles discussed above is at odds with this; it is simply a caveat to all organisations to follow their primary mission of producing creativity, while ensuring that appropriate governance structures support and enable this.

An example of this would be an arts organisation taking a big financial risk by running an expensive show. There is a risk of failure and monetary loss, so should the organisation exercise prudence, minimise the risk, protect its funds and turn down the big artistic opportunity? From a governance perspective, the answer is a resounding 'no'; arts organisations should recognise the need to take these financial risks in order to create opportunities to produce and promote great art. (Risk management is discussed further in **Chapter 7** as a way of mitigating these types of scenarios.)

Furthermore, the arts sector interviewees were clear that the benefits of a good governance framework went beyond merely being compliant with relevant legislation and best practice. For one thing, they found that places producing good art were more likely to have a good governance framework in place. That is not to say that good governance creates good art, but that it is a symptom of a well-run organisation in which good art can flourish.[33] This book resists any attempt to argue that good governance *causes* good art; this would denigrate the creative process. However, it is argued that sufficient awareness of the principles of good corporate governance in the sector is lacking, and that the recognition and application of those principles can support and enable creative enterprises.

Corporate governance needs to be applied with careful consideration of the uniqueness of the arts sector. The uniqueness of the arts sector is well recognised by those who fund it; the existence of the Arts Council and city and county arts offices are the recognition by government and society of this uniqueness.

---

[33] Some attempts have been made in other sectors to show a causal link between organisational performance and good governance (e.g. Opus Executive Partners, "How's Mine Doing? A Review of Boards, Performance and Risk in the Mining Sector" (2011)), but they are inconclusive.

Arts organisations are defined by their artistic merit, values and aims. However, these values and aims can be neither heard nor achieved without the strategic alignment of corporate governance and its role in creating organisations that are fundable and provide good value for stakeholders' money. The 'magic mix' is a confluence of direction by the board, control by management and creativity by the artists, which creates efficiency, cost-effectiveness and achievement of the organisation's aims.

Sustainability

Good corporate governance benefits an organisation's financial sustainability. In co-operation with the Arts Council, the Department of Arts, Heritage and the Gaeltacht is working to ensure that Irish arts organisations continue to receive sufficient funding in the face of ongoing financial cuts from all government sources. Their strategy statement reads: "We will work with stakeholders in the arts community to develop new proposals aimed at building private support of the arts in Ireland exploring philanthropic, sponsorship or endowment fund opportunities."[34]

It is widely accepted that arts organisations should not live on third-party grants alone, but that they should be viable enterprises with other sources of independent income. The concern for building independent sustainability by developing funding sources outside of the Arts Council and city council sources is a core reason for adopting good corporate governance. Well-governed organisations will be more likely to secure non-government funding and will therefore be more sustainable – so the ability of arts organisations to show that they are well governed is essential.

Transparency

Good governance also enables transparency, and funders identify disclosure of information as an important part of good governance. However, transparency is more convincing when it is led by the arts organisation, rather than demanded by its funders. This is clear in the GuideStar "Transparency Report",[35] which, for example, recommends the voluntary disclosure of audited financial statements and corporate information, such as annual

---

[34] Department of Arts, Heritage and the Gaeltacht, *Statement of Strategy 2011–2014* (2011).
[35] GuideStar is a database for non-profits in America. Its "Transparency Report" makes recommendations for good governance within American non-profit organisations. www.guidestar.org.

reports, on organisational websites, and that this information should be updated regularly.[36] GuideStar research has found that if donors had "better information in more transparent and clear formats", they could more easily be encouraged to donate.[37]

Transparency seems straightforward when an organisation is running smoothly and according to plan. It can become problematic when difficulties are encountered, which is when the relationship between management and the board becomes vital for the business. A good, transparent relationship allows problems to be discussed and the whole organisation to get behind resolution of the issues. The board can then decide if and when to communicate problems to external stakeholders. Stakeholders are typically willing to continue to support organisations where problems are known and clearly visible, measures are in place to solve the issues, and controls are planned or implemented to ensure the problems do not recur. However, where problems have been discovered in the wider not-for-profit sector, withdrawal of funding has occurred. "Five community groups lost State funding last year" was the title of a 2011 article in the *Sunday Independent*,[38] which cited audits undertaken on behalf of the government and a subsequent withdrawal of funding due to concerns about how the organisations managed their finances. This need not happen; the Arts Council and other funders will often work with organisations where problems are being encountered and where they are made aware of the issues as soon as they arise. Sometimes they will recommend strengthening the board as a solution to the issues. An observation made in interviewing funders for this book was their universal willingness to work with their funded organisations.

The GuideStar Transparency Report, as introduced above, found that 93% of American non-profits are using their websites to disclose information about their programmes and services. In addition, nearly three-quarters of the organisations provided the names of those serving on their governing boards as well as the names of key management. However, only 43% of the non-profits surveyed posted their annual reports on their websites. Organisations with higher income levels were more likely to make their annual reports available online. The report found that only 13% posted their audited financial statements online, revealing a reluctance to disclose audited financial statements publicly.

---

[36] GuideStar, "Transparency Report. The State of Nonprofit Transparency: Voluntary disclosure practices" (2008).

[37] Ottenhoff, B. and Ulrich, G., "More Money for Good" (GuideStar, 2012).

[38] Sheehan, M., "Five community groups lost State funding last year: Money held back over major concerns", *Irish Independent*, 2 January 2011.

The situation in the Irish non-profit sector is not very different, and the findings of the GuideStar report are equally applicable to Irish arts organisations, particularly its recommendations on how to increase organisational transparency.

The Objectives of this Book

Corporate Governance for the Irish Arts Sector has three aims:

1. Explore the governance frameworks and practices in the arts sector, identifying best practice and what governance standards are actually being used.
2. Identify what governance standards funding institutions expect to see in arts organisations.
3. Examine how funders monitor funded organisations and whether the funding criteria reflect a requirement for good governance practices, including sustainability.

In the midst of these objectives, it is necessary to identify the stakeholders of arts organisations, which include those who fund arts organisations, arts audiences, who can complain loudly if they are not getting good value for their money, and us, the wider community or 'public'.

With that in mind, it is important to address the following questions:

- What are the characteristics of good governance and what does a good governance programme look like?
- How should a good corporate governance framework be defined in the arts sector?
- What will the key benefits be of governance transparency and accountability in the arts sector?
- In the changing landscape for funding in Ireland, will good corporate governance, transparency and accountability affect funding in the arts sector, and what are funding organisations looking for in arts organisations?

Summary

In discussing corporate governance in the Irish arts sector, we first need to define what we mean by 'the arts sector' and 'arts organisations'. For the purpose of this book, the sector is composed of slightly fewer than

1,000 organisations, many of which are small, operating mainly in the non-profit sector. The definition of an arts organisation that we will use is: an organisation receiving some form of grant aid, or outside assistance from the community, in order to facilitate creative output.

These arts organisations need good governance, not only to enjoy the benefits of being well-run and the demonstrated positive effects on artistic output but also because many have non-profit status and will continue to require external funding in order to achieve their visions and goals.

Good governance has very specific advantages for the arts sector. First, it will help the sector as a whole avoid scandals such as those we have suffered in other, 'for-profit' sectors. This is important because almost the entire arts sector depends on at least some external funding – and funders demand value for money. Good, visible governance is clearly beneficial, while negative media publicity arising from any scandals will be damaging. Those interviewed for this book were confident that arts organisations can take risks to achieve great art, recognising that they may sometimes fail in this; however, clear distinctions can be made between a failed artistic attempt and wasted or misappropriated funds. Therefore, the demonstration of good governance assures funders of the proper stewardship of their funds.

Individual arts organisations are in a competitive environment to win funding; good corporate governance, which leads to voluntary transparency and disclosure, will improve their chances of receiving funds. Leading reports addressing the issue of transparency show that while financial statements are frequently not disclosed on organisational websites, such types of disclosure will improve transparency. Similar to the US, transparency in the Irish arts sector is lacking. Improved awareness of the principles of corporate governance could improve organisational transparency. (Note that no distinction is being made between transparency with funders and public transparency; this is because funders are accountable to the public and therefore public accountability is required.)

The Companies Acts and the *UK Corporate Governance Code*, together with the Irish non-profit Governance Code, are widely used and accepted by the sector and its funders. The principles of good governance are largely immutable. Governance programmes may look different in organisations of different sizes, but they will always be founded on the same principles. This means that we can look to the greater body of work on and research into corporate governance from the wider, for-profit sector. We can appropriate best practices from other sectors to ensure that our arts sector, although different, benefits from the same good practices used in all well-governed organisations.

While the principles may be the same, there are particular problems and issues in implementing and maintaining a good governance programme that are specific to arts organisations. For example, arts organisations do not use profit as a primary measure of success. Instead, the quality and impact of the artistic output, or the achievement of values and mission, are often used. These success criteria show that arts organisations need special treatment in the consideration of corporate governance. It is these criteria that will be considered in the next chapter.

Chapter 2

What Does Good Corporate Governance Look Like and Who are the Stakeholders?

The operations of all truly successful arts organisations follow the same simple model: they create wonderful, innovative, and surprising artistic and educational programming ...
Michael Kaiser, *Leading Roles: 50 Questions Every Arts Board Should Ask*

Introduction

This chapter explores what good corporate governance looks like. As discussed in **Chapter 1**, the main principles of corporate governance are set out by the Financial Reporting Council (FRC) in the *UK Corporate Governance Code*, i.e. leadership, effectiveness and accountability.[1] These principles are not very different from those in the Governance Code for the Irish non-profit sector, a document that describes itself as "for the sector by the sector",[2] and which describes the principles of good governance as: providing leadership, exercising control, being transparent and accountable, working effectively, and behaving with integrity.

But what are the issues arising from the operation and organisation of arts organisations? Are there issues that are particularly relevant for arts organisations? These questions, addressed below, represent the questions most often asked by arts organisations of their financial advisors.

And, why are we concerned about corporate governance in the first place? Who is it for? Who are its customers? Addressing these questions using stakeholder theory will identify the taxpayer as the ultimate, main funder of arts organisations. Because in understanding who 'pays the piper', we can understand who 'calls the tune', and arts organisations will be enabled to address the

---

[1] Financial Reporting Council, *The UK Corporate Governance Code* (2012).
[2] The *Governance Code for Community, Voluntary and Charitable Organisations in Ireland* (2011) (the 'Governance Code', see www.governancecode.ie).

concerns of the tax-paying public. We can see an example of this in the Central Remedial Clinic scandal of 2013/14, when the government, representing the public, stepped in and called the board to account for its actions.

The Principles of Corporate Governance

The Financial Reporting Council (FRC) defines a principle of corporate governance that applies to all organisations: "The purpose of corporate governance is to facilitate effective, entrepreneurial and prudent management that can deliver the long-term success of the company."[3] Good corporate governance is characterised by the following: complying with the Companies Acts, having a well-run board, effective internal control, an effective decision-making process and clear vision and mission statements. The alignment of the board, management team and stakeholders' expectations is also characteristic of a well-governed organisation. Adhering to the main principles of corporate governance is fundamental to delivering long-term success.

Arts organisations serve their organisational vision and they serve their stakeholders. Their achievements are not measurable by profit alone, and where those organisations are constituted as companies limited by guarantee, or having charitable status, they do not necessarily seek to make any profits. Arts organisations, therefore, have an additional component to their governance principles: to produce great art. Many of those interviewed for this book identified what they referred to as a 'magic mix'. Interviewees, while respecting the need for governance, were clear that artistic merit should be the main driver of well-governed arts organisations; the artistic idea and artistic creativity must come first. If good corporate governance follows, this alignment constitutes a 'magic mix'.

Compliance with the Companies Acts

For all incorporated arts organisations, full compliance with the Irish Companies Acts is a cornerstone of good governance. The principles embodied in company law provide a basic framework for well-run boards of directors, effective internal controls and proactive management. Interviewees, representing funders and fundees, cited their full compliance with the Irish Companies Acts as the primary evidence of good corporate governance.

---

[3] Financial Reporting Council, *The UK Corporate Governance Code* (2012).

Many medium and small-sized arts organisations, such as art galleries, theatres and resource organisations,[4] are companies limited by guarantee. The basic requirements of Irish company law, to have proper books of account, a board of directors and annual general meetings, fully apply. (These requirements are detailed in **Chapter 5**.) Appointing a Company Secretary charged with Companies Acts compliance is the minimum that a prudent organisation needs to do and is good practice for all arts organisations.

A Well-run Board of Directors

A well-run and effective board of directors is a prerequisite for good governance. (**Chapter 4** describes board effectiveness in detail.) Boards should set a clear and effective organisational strategy, aligned with the organisation's vision, mission and goals. The arts practitioners and stakeholders interviewed for this book held that where organisational difficulties are observed by funders or stakeholders, the first approach for the organisation is to 'start with the board'. They observed that, in many instances, problems began at board level and differences or conflicts at board level would permeate through the organisation. In many cases, observable organisational breakdowns are a direct result of breakdowns of coordination within the board. (**Chapter 6** further addresses the boards of arts organisations.)

For organisations incorporated under the Companies Acts, the minimum number of directors is two and the maximum is determined by the articles of association for the individual company. A small organisation can have as few as two directors, which may be sufficient when it is incorporated, but as it grows it can increase its numbers, adding more expertise and diversity to the board as required.

Effective Internal Control

'Internal control' generally refers to the *process* by which an organisation is managed and governed. It includes the whole system of controls, both financial and operational, which have been established by management in order to carry out the business of the organisation in an orderly manner. These include bank reconciliations, segregation of duties in relation to spending

---

[4] Resource organisations are representative organisations that provide supports to their members, such as information and HR resources. They are also a collective voice for the organisations they represent.

and receiving money and the keeping of proper financial records. One of the main purposes of the system of controls is also to safeguard the assets of the organisation and to secure, as far as possible, the accuracy and reliability of its records.[5] The controls therefore include adherence to company policies and are designed to improve operational efficiency.

My research found that internal controls were an area little discussed by arts organisations. While funders cannot implement internal controls, for small organisations they usually require that the organisation incorporate as a statutory company with a company bank account. Lodgement of grant monies is usually made to the bank account of the incorporated entity. From the funder's perspective this ensures that the money provided is designated solely for the business of the funded organisation. A concern of the Arts Council is how it can satisfy itself that grantee organisations are "legally fit to receive Arts Council monies",[6] which is manifested in the care taken by the Arts Council in its assessment of governance standards prior to grant-giving.

For large organisations and for larger grants, some funding bodies will carry out due diligence testing and reviews, which includes the evaluation of the quality of the board. Funders may employ professionals to carry out a formal due diligence on the organisation it proposes to fund. The due diligence review can include a full review of financial statements for the last number of years (usually three). A due diligence review examines:

- key control reconciliations;
- the market environment;
- budgets and forecasts;
- the organisation's pipeline of future business, and its track record of successful delivery of services or products in the immediate past; and
- the efficiency and effectiveness of the board and of the management team.

A review of internal controls will provide assurances on the achievement of objectives in the following categories:

- effectiveness and efficiency of operations, including the quality of the management team;

---

[5] Definition adapted by the author from *Coopers & Lybrand Manual of Auditing* (3rd edition) (1981), and COSO (Committee of Sponsoring Organisations of the Treadway Commission, www.COSO.org). The use of these older references is to highlight the existence of some basic definitions prior to the current corporate governance scandals.
[6] Arts Council Consultation Process. Interactions.

- reliability of financial reporting and controls over the accuracy of financial information; and
- compliance with applicable laws and regulations, including the Companies Acts and the organisation's articles of association.

For larger grants there may be milestones to be met before the grant monies are given. Sometimes funding is given in tranches when the organisation achieves the goals set by the funder. In this way, governance is being set by the funders, who request that arts organisations improve their internal controls before applying for grant aid.

Effective Decision-making Processes

Effective decision making is highly important as it should permeate many aspects of the board's governance of the organisation. Many boards find it useful to set out criteria for how they will make decisions, how issues will be put on the agenda, discussed, agreed and minuted, as well as how decisions will be followed up so that the board can be confident they are completed to its satisfaction.

The strength of the board and executive management team, and their mix of skills and expertise, is an important factor in a well-governed entity. However, even with a balanced and skilled team the decision-making process is vital, as is the process of exercising judgement. According to the 2012 report "Enhancing Board Oversight":

> "Corporate governance is enhanced when directors improve their ability to exercise an appropriate level of scepticism and actively engage with management. Entities and their key stakeholders are better served when directors effectively challenge management's judgements, explicitly consider alternative perspectives, and engage management in frank and open discussions."[7]

The same report provides a model of a good decision-making process, as shown in **Figure 2.1** below.

A good and visible decision-making process not only avoids bad decisions but makes the group conscious and observant of conflicts of interest. A good decision-making process identifies the decision to be made by the board on the agenda, as well as identifying the potential for conflict of interest. The chairman

---

[7] KPMG LLP *et al.*, "Enhancing Board Oversight: Avoiding Judgment Traps and Biases" (Committee of Sponsoring Organisations of the Treadway Commission, 2012).

Figure 2.1   **A Good Decision-making Process**

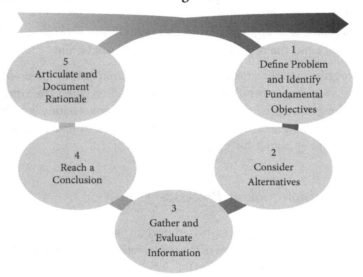

Source: KPMG LLP et al. (2012)

requests any declarations of conflicts of interest, and the board allows the relevant or conflicted board member to excuse themselves from the meeting for that item or to refrain from voting on the matter.

A further factor that can affect decision making is 'groupthink', a term coined by the social psychologist Irving L. Janis in 1972.[8] Groupthink is an insidious problem which can hinder good decisions from being carried and put into effect, in this case by a board. It occurs when the group puts pressure on its members to agree, and as a consequence a poor or unchallenged decision is made by the group. This can happen where there is one dominant group member or members. Because the members feel under pressure to act in agreement, the group decisions typically lack objectivity. Members of the group act to achieve consensus and suspend their own independent judgement and decision making. When members of a board are similar in background, when the decision-making process is not clear and when the rules are not set out in advance, the board can more easily fall into the error of groupthink, leading to bad or poor decisions.

Groupthink is counterbalanced not only by a good mix of people on the board (see **Chapter 6**) but also by the board's own decision-making process,

---

[8] Janis, I.L., *Groupthink: Psychological Studies of Policy Decisions and Fiascoes* (2nd edition) (Wadsworth, 1982).

which should be evident and well explained to everyone on the board. A conscious decision-making process, such as the one illustrated above, will enable a board to be effective; its decisions will be clear and the organisation will be able to execute the decisions.

Vision and Mission

The organisation's vision should be embodied in its mission statement, which is set out by the board of directors. A mission statement defines and describes an organisation's purpose, and provides it with a 'roadmap' to the future, enabling those working in the organisation to have goals for its achievement. It also provides stakeholders with a clear view of what the organisation is about, its planned contribution to its members or stakeholders and its values. A mission statement will enable the board to set strategy to achieve the organisation's goals.

Organisations frequently develop their vision and mission statements in collaboration with all employees, as employee input improves awareness of the vision and mission. Communicating the vision and mission statements is easier when their aspirations belong to everyone in the organisation.

An example of a mission statement is that of the Irish Museum of Modern Art (IMMA), which states that its mission is: "to foster within society an awareness, understanding and involvement in the visual arts through policies and programmes which are excellent, innovative and inclusive." Another example, this one longer and more detailed, is from the Museum of Modern Art (MoMA) in New York:[9]

EXAMPLE: MISSION STATEMENT – MoMA, NEW YORK[10]

Mission Statement

Founded in 1929 as an educational institution, The Museum of Modern Art is dedicated to being the foremost museum of modern art in the world.

---

[9] Author's note: this is not to imply that the MoMA mission statement is better than the IMMA mission statement – any comparison is to show their different purposes.

[10] www.moma.org (accessed November 2013).

Through the leadership of its Trustees and staff, The Museum of Modern Art manifests this commitment by establishing, preserving, and documenting a permanent collection of the highest order that reflects the vitality, complexity and unfolding patterns of modern and contemporary art; by presenting exhibitions and educational programs of unparalleled significance; by sustaining a library, archives, and conservation laboratory that are recognized as international centers of research; and by supporting scholarship and publications of preeminent intellectual merit.

Central to The Museum of Modern Art's mission is the encouragement of an ever-deeper understanding and enjoyment of modern and contemporary art by the diverse local, national, and international audiences that it serves.

To achieve its goals The Museum of Modern Art recognizes:

- That modern and contemporary art originated in the exploration of the ideals and interests generated in the new artistic traditions that began in the late nineteenth century and continue today.
- That modern and contemporary art transcend national boundaries and involve all forms of visual expression, including painting and sculpture, drawings, prints and illustrated books, photography, architecture and design, and film and video, as well as new forms yet to be developed or understood, that reflect and explore the artistic issues of the era.
- That these forms of visual expression are an open-ended series of arguments and counter arguments that can be explored through exhibitions and installations and are reflected in the Museum's varied collection.
- That it is essential to affirm the importance of contemporary art and artists if the Museum is to honor the ideals with which it was founded and to remain vital and engaged with the present.
- That this commitment to contemporary art enlivens and informs our evolving understanding of the traditions of modern art.
- That to remain at the forefront of its field, the Museum must have an outstanding professional staff and must periodically reevaluate itself, responding to new ideas and initiatives with insight,

> imagination, and intelligence. The process of reevaluation is mandated by the Museum's tradition, which encourages openness and a willingness to evolve and change.
>
> In sum, The Museum of Modern Art seeks to create a dialogue between the established and the experimental, the past and the present, in an environment that is responsive to the issues of modern and contemporary art, while being accessible to a public that ranges from scholars to young children.

Having outlined what it looks like, we will now consider what drives and influences good governance.

Identifying Stakeholders – and Why they are Important

A review of 'stakeholder theory' will explain some of the dynamics in the Irish arts sector. Stakeholder theory "focuses on the demands of external groups that can affect the organisation and how managers respond to these groups".[11] Stakeholder theory can therefore be used to identify the stakeholders who have an interest in corporate governance in the arts sector. Pragmatically, however, we just need to identify the dynamic between arts organisations and their funders, and the key drivers of this relationship.

The Arts Council, by far the main funder of Irish arts organisations, is funded by the Irish government, and therefore by the Irish taxpayer. (The importance of this funding being at 'arm's length' is discussed in **Chapter 7**.) As the Irish taxpayer is the main funder of Irish arts and culture, this also means that the taxpayer is the main stakeholder in our arts organisations. The implications of this fact are important for the arts sector. Where it is perceived that grants are given to organisations from taxpayer money, it is justifiable for arts organisations to be accountable to those taxpayers. Because taxpayers are the largest group of stakeholders, in recessionary times, with grant-giving being cut back, taxpayers demand more value for money and transparency around the expenditure processes. Funding and pay cuts are being made everywhere; in this context it is

---

[11] Mitchell, R. *et al.*, "Toward a Theory of Stakeholder Identification and Salience: Defining the Principle of Who and What Really Counts" (1997) Vol. 22, No. 4, *Academy of Management Review*, 853–86.

reasonable to expect that the public would also question value for money in their funding for the arts. This led to the founding of the National Campaign for the Arts[12] in 2009, and the vigorous debates about the importance of the arts in society that followed.

It is useful to recognise taxpayers as stakeholders of Irish arts organisations in this way. Much academic research has been done on stakeholder theory and it can be used here as a helpful tool for understanding the need for corporate governance from the point of view of the funder. The research suggests a dynamic relationship between stakeholders and funded organisations, meaning that when the dynamic shifts (for example, when a long and deep recession hits the economy), the relationship between the stakeholder and fundees also changes dynamically and fundamentally.

R. Edward Freeman defines stakeholders as "any group or individual who can affect or is affected by the achievement of the organisation's objectives".[13] Freeman recently updated the definition to include organisational *failure*: "these are groups and individuals who have a stake in the success or failure of a business".[14] As stakeholders, Irish taxpayers therefore have a stake in the success or failure of our arts organisations. So, what happens when the dynamic changes?

Whenever an external force like the global recession occurs, the relationship between the organisation and its stakeholders inevitably changes. A dynamic model of the altered relationship, based on power, legitimacy and urgency, is postulated by Mitchell *et al.* as follows: power to influence the organisation; legitimacy of the stakeholder's relationship with the organisation; and urgency of the stakeholder's claim on the organisation. Paul Dunn argues that: "When stakeholders have two of these attributes, management can no longer be passive."[15]

Therefore, management and boards of arts organisations now need to address the needs and demands of their stakeholders, or risk going out of business. Those stakeholders are clamouring urgently, they have a legitimate reason (shortage of funds and a demand of value for money), and they

---

[12] "The National Campaign for the Arts is a volunteer-led, grass roots movement that makes the case for the arts in Ireland", ncfa.ie/about (accessed May 2013).

[13] R. Edward Freeman, cited in Mitchell *et al.*, "Toward a Theory of Stakeholder Identification and Salience: Defining the Principle of Who and What Really Counts" (1997) Vol. 22, No. 4, *Academy of Management Review*, 853–86.

[14] Freeman R. *et al.*, *Stakeholder Theory: The State of the Art* (Cambridge University Press, 2010).

[15] Dunn, P., "Strategic Responses by a Nonprofit when a Donor becomes Tainted" (2010) Vol. 39, No. 1, *Nonprofit and Voluntary Sector Quarterly*, 102–23.

have the power to cut funding. At present, Irish taxpayers see themselves as the ultimate funders of arts organisations and there is an urgent need to save money. Therefore, the Irish public are the ultimate decision makers, and they require good governance. We can expect that transparency and accountability will need to be demonstrated, and good stewardship of tax-payer money will need to be shown. The numerous reports from the art sector on their value-adding and employment capability demonstrate this trend.[16] Due to these trends, the landscape for funding is changing, and funders and arts organisations alike are focused on better governance. For example, many organisations are adopting the Governance Code referred to above or are requesting 'governance audits'.

Against the background of a severe shortage of funding available for Irish arts organisations, the salience (or prioritisation of who and what really counts) of the Irish taxpayer highlights the purpose and the stringency of corporate governance standards. Furthermore, servicing the interests of the taxpayer must drive the governance requirements for integrity, account-ability, transparency and value for money.[17]

Stakeholder Salience

Stakeholders, in this case Irish taxpayers, have become even more important, and taxpayers are more vocal about questioning public expenditure in the wake of the global recession. Thus, we can reasonably expect the voice of the Irish taxpayer to be louder and to carry more weight, to have greater 'salience' in the decision-making process. Stakeholder salience is "the degree to which managers give priority to competing stakeholder claims".[18] In this context, it goes beyond the mere identification of stakeholders and has shifted from the public as audience and spectators to the public as taxpayers, who seek to make funded organisations accountable in difficult financial circumstances. All of these circumstances indicate a severe shortage of funding and increased competition for shrinking funds.

---

[16] For example, the Arts Council, "Assessment of Economic Impact of the Arts in Ireland" (November 2009) by Indecon International Economic Consultants.

[17] *Ibid.*

[18] Mitchell, R. *et al.*, "Toward a Theory of Stakeholder Identification and Salience: Defining the Principle of Who and What Really Counts" (1997) Vol. 22, No. 4, *Academy of Management Review*, 853–86.

At a time when Irish cultural organisations are braced for ongoing and significant grant cuts, fundraising from a variety of sources may well be the only way for those institutions to maintain their status. This could mean that the Arts Council may shift from being such a dominant funder of many organisations. The Arts Council is already encouraging arts organisations to diversify funding through initiatives to enable fundraising.[19]

The Business Model and Organisational Sustainability

'Organisational sustainability' refers to the ability of an organisation to stay in business and to fulfil its mission in the medium and long term. In order for an organisation to achieve this, it must have the following: a sustainable business model, which includes a reasonably stable source of funding; willing and appropriately qualified board members and management, and a product or service that is in demand. Many arts organisations are dependent on annual grants, either from the Arts Council, the city or county councils, or other sources. This dependency creates uncertainty in the business models of many Irish arts organisations, which have no other sources of income, making them completely dependent on a single source of external funding. It was this observation that initially prompted the study of corporate governance in Irish arts organisations, leading to this book. It is becoming increasingly evident that these organisations need to diversify their sources of income in order to survive and to continue as going concerns. In restructuring their funding models and looking for new sources of income, such organisations first need to ensure that their corporate governance is visible and transparent.

The dependency on uncertain annual funding leads to a conundrum that is itself problematic in terms of governance. For example, when embarking on a three-year programme, an organisation and its board would need to make decisions for an unknown future. Typically, the executives proposing any plans or projects whose duration is expected to be longer than one year need to address unknown funding sources and the uncertain sustainability of their organisation. That uncertainty can lead to the organisation only

---

[19] For example, fundraising programmes such as the Arts Council's RAISE programme. **Chapter 6** discusses RAISE and other initiatives to build fundraising capacity through planning and implementing fundraising programmes.

taking on short-term projects, and the organisation may suffer from a lack of long-term planning and a reluctance to initiate longer-term projects.

The solution to this disconnected planning is for arts organisations to create new and diverse sources of funding, and the first step towards this is to demonstrate excellent corporate governance structures. The next step is to put in place funding for a longer term, for example, funding approval for a three-year programme would allow the organisation to plan for future endeavours with a degree of certainty.

Arts organisations in these circumstances will benefit from a cohesive, functional board charged with strategic thinking. The importance of the board and its understanding of strategy in the face of a business model dependent on short-term funding is clear. In these circumstances, the board needs to focus on funding and funder relationships to ensure ongoing funding for programmes which span a number of funding years.

Summary

The conversation on corporate governance quickly moves to how arts organisations are organised, led and managed. Although Irish arts organisations are a mixed group of incorporated and unincorporated, for-profit and non-profit entities with and without charitable status, they mostly receive a large portion of their funding from external sources, which in Ireland is ultimately the taxpayer.

The Arts Council is the largest funder of Irish arts organisations. Because they are government-funded, the Irish taxpayer is the main stakeholder in arts organisations. The changing concerns of the taxpayer following the economic downturn and resulting money shortage therefore impacts on arts organisations. Transparency and the demonstration of good governance will help to ensure that the sector maintains its flow of funding. The implementation of governance programmes in individual organisations and the main pertinent legislation guidelines and accounting processes will be discussed next in the context of implementing corporate governance structures in arts organisations.

Organisations in the arts sector are usually set up and run by artists and arts managers, all of whom work with the best intentions and a genuine passion for what they do. These structures have to date usually been adequate. However, budgets are always tight and the uncertainty of funding has made thinking and planning for much beyond a one-year cycle a luxury.

In a landscape that is changing for arts organisations, there are two options:

- try to stop the change (this is usually addressed by campaigns to stop the funding cuts);[20] or
- change and adapt the arts organisation itself.

In later chapters we examine a more 'joined-up thinking' approach within arts organisations, where governance is embedded in the organisation and the board dynamic supports a conscious effort to drive the organisation's vision and purpose.

[20] Such as the National Campaign for the Arts (NCFA), www.ncfa.ie.

Chapter 3

Governance Frameworks for Arts Organisations

'No surprises' is one of the most important principles of good corporate governance.
International Finance Corporation,
World Bank Group (2009)

Introduction

This chapter answers the question: "Where can I look at corporate governance practices and frameworks in order to find a suitable programme for my organisation?"

We have discussed the arts sector and attempted to define it within the cultural sector and to place it in an Irish context, identifying key issues that arts organisations encounter. This chapter deals with arts organisations as individual entities, and suggests definitions for 'the arts' and for the different types of arts organisation. It also identifies useful accounting practices and structures, and current initiatives from the business sectors that are applicable to arts organisations.

Defining arts organisations is not straightforward. As we have seen, such organisations may be incorporated entities or non-incorporated; they may have charitable status or simply define themselves as 'non-profits'; they may be limited by guarantee of the members or be private limited companies; many are in receipt of Arts Council or other grants or benefits-in-kind, and some are sole traders. In this chapter, the organisations are grouped according to their corporate governance needs in order to discuss appropriate frameworks for their corporate governance programmes.

Definition and Characteristics of Governance Frameworks for Arts Organisations

There is general agreement that identifiable corporate governance frameworks do exist in the sector. This is partly because many arts organisations are incorporated entities and fall under the regulations and governance frameworks for small and medium-sized organisations. Broad guidelines for corporate governance are also identified in legislation and guidelines, such as the *UK Corporate Governance Code* and in best practices defined by the Office of the Director of Corporate Enforcement (ODCE). Non-profit organisations (of which arts organisations are a subset) have a further refinement of governance structures as identified in the Charities Act 2009. However, there is still a need for arts organisations to customise that framework to their own particular needs, and to use it well.

This chapter will explore whether there is awareness among arts organisations that demonstrating good corporate governance through strategic alignment and transparency is important; and whether there is sufficient awareness of what this means in practice and operationally.

There needs to be more awareness, simply because better corporate governance leads to more funding. The funders of arts organisations are clear that better-run organisations have better funding prospects and their funding application forms seek to discover this.[1]

The standards discussed by arts sector interviewees were:

- the Charities Act;
- the *UK Corporate Governance Code* (formerly the *Combined Code*);
- the *Governance Code for Community, Voluntary and Charitable Organisations in Ireland* ('the Governance Code');
- the *Code of Practice for State Bodies* ('the Code of Practice'); and
- the *SWiFT Code* (which is described as having the primary objective to "facilitate external assessment of Corporate Governance performance").[2]

Although frameworks for corporate governance do exist in Ireland, and can be identified by the sector, many of the governance structures are non-mandatory. All incorporated entities must comply with the Companies

---

[1] The Arts Council, the Ireland Funds and Dublin City Council, for example, specifically require organisations to include details of their boards and request financial statements and board minutes.

[2] National Standards Authority of Ireland, *Code of Practice for Corporate Governance Assessment in Ireland* (2010) NSAI Standards, SWiFT 3000.

Acts and with employment legislation, but neither the governance codes nor the charities Statement of Recommended Practice (SORP) on accounting are compulsory in Ireland. In the UK, however, the SORP is mandatory, and there is working legislation for the regulation of charities, such as the Charities Act 2006.

A summary of the key issues that make non-profit organisations different is adapted from a table by Prospectus Management Consultants at Table 3.1 below.[3]

The differences between non-profit arts organisations and for-profit organisations can be seen clearly in the table above. Non-profit arts organisations are accountable to a large number of stakeholders, and their primary

Table 3.1   **Non-profit and For-profit Arts Organisations: Key Differences in Corporate Governance Issues**

Comparison	Non-profit Arts Organisations	For-profit organisations
Ownership	Stakeholder	Shareholder
Accountability	Stakeholders, artists, audience, funders, taxpayers	Shareholder
Organisational objective/ motivation	Artistic endeavour	Profit
Remuneration	Paid staff, volunteers and interns	Paid staff
Liability	Limited liability for the vast majority of non-profit and arts organisations	Mainly limited, but unlimited for some private organisations
Finance funding	Donors/government	Customers/shareholders
Shareholders'/ stakeholder rights	Stakeholders have fewer rights	Shareholders have strong and defined rights with respect to their financial input and/or shareholdings

[3] Adapted from Prospectus, "For-Profit Versus Nonprofit: Key Differences in Corporate Governance Issues" (Prospectus Management Consultants, 2006).

concern is with *values* rather than profit. Their motivation is to produce art, and to foster artistic endeavour, and in doing so they necessarily differ from typical for-profit organisations. By comparison, for-profit companies have shareholders who are able to hold corporate directors and officers accountable. In the non-profit organisation the mechanism for stakeholders, rather than shareholders, to hold the organisation accountable is less clear and more difficult to enforce. In non-profit arts organisations, the longer list of stakeholders, artists, audience, funders and taxpayers applies; there is less likelihood of direct challenge from this more disparate group.

A key difference is that non-profit arts organisations must gain the public's trust in order to obtain public funds; compared to for-profit organisations, many of which are judged primarily on their share-price performance. The key issues of values and trust will drive the corporate governance of the not-for-profit sector and of non-profit arts organisations in particular.

The Charities Act

Many arts organisations have charitable status, as granted by Revenue, and can be defined as 'charities'. The difficulty with the definition of a charity and a non-profit organisation is discussed in the INKEx report referred to in **Chapter 1**. This report notes that arts organisations may be non-profits and may have charitable status, and therefore should be regulated as charities.[4]

In Ireland, however, the implementation of the Charities Act 2009 has been delayed and is currently being recommenced.[5] The Act establishes a Charities Regulatory Authority (CRA), which will keep a register of charities, and charities will be required to submit an annual statement of accounts to the Authority. The register of charitable organisations will provide important statistics on the sector, and it will allow the sector to be segmented into meaningful groups (e.g. arts organisations). This data will be kept up to date, as a further provision of the Act stipulates that all charities, regardless of legal structure, will be required to submit an annual activity report to the Authority. Most arts organisations fall within the definition of a

---

[4] Irish Nonprofits Knowledge Exchange, "Irish Nonprofits: What do we know?" (January 2012).
[5] At the ICTR Annual Conference on 8 November 2012, Minister of State at the Department of Justice, Equality and Defence, Kathleen Lynch TD, speaking on behalf of the then Minister for Justice, Equality and Defence, Alan Shatter TD, told the conference that Minister Shatter was to publish a consultation on his plans for bringing the Charities Act 2009 into force (www.mondaq.com, accessed 14 December 2012).

'charity' for the purposes of the Act.[6] The delay in implementing the Charities Act therefore affects many arts organisations. More importantly, it leaves the non-profit sector unregulated.

It is useful to detail the concerns and stipulations of the Charities Act which are relevant to arts organisations. Although the Act is not yet operational, a consultation process prior to its implementation has commenced. The legislation's concerns affect arts organisations and provide indicators of current good practice in Ireland. It also takes into account the views of the stakeholders of charitable organisations and therefore can be expected to provide a reasonable consensus among the non-profit sector on required regulation and best practices.

Further provisions of the Act regulate fundraising activity, including the requirement to obtain permits for all types of fundraising. The Act also provides for greater transparency, requiring details of fundraising activity and expenditure to be shown in annual accounts.

The Impact of the Charities Act on Financial Statements

The potential impact of the Charities Act on financial statements has been discussed by Teresa Harrington in her book, *Accounting and Reporting by Charities in the Republic of Ireland.*[7] Although the Charities Act requires an annual activity report to be submitted to the Charities Regulatory Authority, the Act falls short of providing direction on disclosure in accounts, particularly disclosure of income-generating expenses, or on administration of the charity. As Harrington points out: "In the Republic of Ireland there is currently no specific format for the accounts and reports of charities."[8]

The lack of uniform disclosure formats means that the financial statements of arts organisations may not adhere to similar disclosure requirements. This makes for difficult and potentially inaccurate comparisons of financial statements of arts organisations (and charities in general). This lack of comparability and uniformity has significant implications for the corporate governance of these organisations, particularly as stakeholders cannot compare the financial statements of similar arts organisations in detail. For example, ratios

---

[6] Section 3(11)(k) states that "charitable purpose" includes "the advancement of the arts, culture, heritage or sciences".

[7] Harrington, T., *Accounting and Reporting by Charities in the Republic of Ireland* (Chartered Accountants Ireland, 2011).

[8] *Ibid.*

are distorted by the inconsistent inclusion of cost and revenue items; and, in Ireland, some organisations are partially compliant with SORP while others ignore it. It is expected that the new Financial Reporting Standard, FRS102, which is applicable from January 2015, will improve financial reporting by arts organisations, and this is discussed below.

Annual Returns and Annual Activity Reports

Since there was extensive consultation prior to the commencement of the enactment of the Charities Act 2009, it is reasonable to conclude that the sector is in broad agreement with its main requirements. The relevant requirements of the Act in relation to financial statements are as follows:

- Charities are required to issue annual returns and activity reports to the new Charities Regulatory Authority. However, as detailed above, there is no prescribed format for these reports.
- For larger charities, audited accounts will be required for income above a prescribed threshold of €500,000 (section 50(2)).
- An examination of accounts will be required for companies with income below the prescribed threshold. Charities with total income/expenditure of less than €10,000 in a given year will not be required to submit audited or examined accounts, but will have to include a summary of their finances in their annual activity report. The Act provides that the regulations can vary the level and detail of information required from different classes of charities, e.g. smaller or larger charities.

Although the Act prescribes annual activity reports and stipulates circumstances where audits are required, it does not comment on the content or disclosure of these activity reports. Best practices for these important disclosures are examined below.

The Statement of Recommended Practice (SORP) and its Benefits

The importance of clear and consistent financial statements for arts organisations cannot be underestimated. Financial statements should be clear and easily understood so that stakeholders can use them to determine how an organisation is using granted or donated funds. The financial statements should show good governance and good stewardship of funds, while also showing accountability and transparency.

As described above, the lack of uniformity in applying accounting standards means that no matter how hard an arts organisation tries to produce excellent and understandable financial statements, those financial statements may not look at all like those of comparable arts organisations. Furthermore, because recommended accounting standards for non-profits are optional in Ireland, the accounting practices do not compel arts organisations to produce comparable financial statements. In addition, neither standard accounting practices nor specific accounting disclosures are required by the Charities Act, beyond the filing of financial statements.

Best practices for accounting and disclosure by charities are set out in the UK's "Accounting and Reporting by Charities: Statement of Recommended Practice (Effective 1 January 2015)". Some of the provisions of this statement of recommended practice (SORP) were used in the Irish Charities Act of 2009.[9] The recommended accounting practices and disclosures are described by Teresa Harrington: "Irish charities, in the absence of regulations governing the financial reporting requirements of charities, may consider the requirements of the SORP as representing best practice."[10] Harrington goes on to describe how to reflect best practice in the financial statements; she uses the UK SORP and attaches a template of the statement of financial activities (SOFA) from it. The implication is that the UK SORP will comply with the Irish Charities Act and that it may be used as best practice for disclosure in Irish financial statements; but most of all its adoption will move the sector towards uniform accounting practices, thereby allowing comparisons and improved understanding of financial statements.

Nonetheless, the Charities Act does provide for statements of financial activities. This applies to all arts organisations that are defined as charities, and is described by Harrington as follows:

> "The basic objective of the Statement of Financial Activities (SOFA) is to bring together all of the funds available to the charity and demonstrate how these have been used to meet the charity's objectives. The SOFA should clearly show all of the activities undertaken by the charity and the terms used to describe the activities should mirror those used to describe the incoming resources as far as possible."[11]

(The recommended 'Statement of Financial Activities' is reproduced in **Appendix 5**.)

---

[9] Compliance with this SORP is not mandatory in Ireland.

[10] Harrington, T., *Accounting and Reporting by Charities in the Republic of Ireland* (Chartered Accountants Ireland, 2011).

[11] *Ibid.*

Full compliance with the SORP is rare amongst Irish arts organisations; this book strongly encourages compliance as a means of making the financial statements of non-profit organisations in the arts sector more understandable.

The SORP takes into account the uniqueness and nature of the transactions of arts organisations and requires the disclosure of all incoming resources. It also requires the disclosure of the costs of generating those incoming resources. In this way, potential funders can see the impact of grants and donations given to the organisation. They can also see how much of the donated funds are spent on the organisation's objectives, on administrating the organisation and on fundraising. The effect of this is twofold: first, if stakeholders can see how their money is being spent, they can judge the organisation's efficiency and effectiveness in administering the funds; secondly, funders of the sector can clearly see the administration and fundraising cost ratio for the organisation.

As yet in Ireland, there is no agreement on what a well-run non-profit might look like in terms of running costs. Some non-profits are asked by donors that the entire donation (particularly for charitable donations) be spent on the charitable cause. However, this neither recognises nor values the contribution of professionals working in the recipient organisations. Funders should expect that a reasonable portion of their donation would be spent on running the organisation (a "reasonable portion" can be defined by industry comparisons and norms).

In the arts sector, arts professionals should be adequately remunerated and organisations will incur administration and running costs. The stakeholders of arts organisations should be entitled to see how their funds are being spent, i.e. the ratio of those funds spent on artistic output and on administering that output. In Ireland, little discussion of these ratios takes place. Moreover, those discussions are not being enabled by clear disclosures on financial statements, or by adequate comparisons of arts organisations' financial statements. The adoption of consistent accounting practices would enable such transparency.

Funders report that they frequently have issues with the quality and depth of disclosures in the financial statements of arts organisations. To address this, the Arts Council has issued template documents for arts organisations that demonstrate better financial disclosure to small and mid-sized arts organisations (see **Appendix 9**). Among small and mid-sized organisations, the cost of better disclosure is sometimes cited as a deterrent. Studies show, however, that better disclosure leads to better funding opportunities. In light of the current difficult financial circumstances, improved quality and transparency of financial reporting should be seen as a prerequisite for funding.

Accounting for Arts Organisations that are Private Companies

Most arts organisations are publicly accountable because they receive grants, and some additionally have charitable status and, as discussed above, it is recommended that these organisations adopt the Charities SORP.

Irish arts organisations that are incorporated would now adopt the Financial Reporting Standard 102 (FRS 102). Note that up to 31 December 2014, the "International Financial Reporting Standards for Small and Medium-sized Entities (SMEs)" applied.[12] The IFRS for SMEs defined itself as a self-contained standard designed to meet the needs and capabilities of SMEs. It was designed to be less complex for implementation in SMEs, and topics not relevant for SMEs were omitted. However, from 1 January 2014, this accounting standard is being transitioned to a new accounting standard called Financial Reporting Standard 102 (FRS 102). All companies where FRS 102 applies must be compliant by 1 January 2015. The main issues for non-profits (called "public benefit entities" (PBEs) in the FRS) are described below.

Accounting for incoming resources, for example donations legacies and donated services, are called "non-exchange transactions" (NETs), has changed and specific rules now apply. Receipts from NETs are accounted for as follows:

- If no future performance conditions are required, account for these immediately in income.
- If future performance conditions will apply, account for these in income when the conditions are met.
- If the resources are received in advance of the conditions being met, treat as a liability.[13]

Arts organisations may also need to value and measure their fixed assets more exactly, as FRS 102 requires recognition criteria. The following recognition criteria must be applied in order to determine whether an asset can be reported:

- there must be probable future economic benefits flowing to the entity; and
- its cost must be reliably measured.[14]

---

[12] International Financial Reporting Standards, 2013.
[13] Adapted from Kirk, R., *A Practical Guide to New UK and Irish GAAP* (Chartered Accountants Ireland, 2014).
[14] *Ibid.*

FRS 102 also contains changes in relation to concessionary loans and to public benefit entity combinations or mergers.

Meanwhile, SORP 33 on charities is revised, as FRS 102 will be generally accepted accounting practice (GAAP) in Ireland.

The Code of Practice for the Governance of State Bodies

Where arts organisations are funded by state bodies, the *Code of Practice for the Governance of State Bodies* ('the Code of Practice'), those State funding bodies usually expect the main provisions of the Code of Practice to be in place. The Code of Practice provides a framework for the application of corporate governance best practice in both commercial and non-commercial state bodies.[15] The first set of guidelines on state body corporate governance, entitled *State Bodies Guidelines*, was issued by the Department of Finance in March 1992, with an update in October 2001 and a further update in 2009.

The Code of Practice is the current standard for Irish state bodies, and therefore is an indicator of best practice for those bodies. Interestingly and reassuringly, it shares some of the principles of the *Governance Code for Community, Voluntary and Charitable Organisations* ('the Governance Code') and it quotes from the *Combined Code* (updated in 2012 and renamed the *UK Corporate Governance Code*).

The Code of Practice defines corporate governance as "the systems and procedures by which enterprises are directed and managed". It identifies taxpayers as the main stakeholder group and outlines specific duties of state bodies:

"State bodies must serve the interests of the taxpayer, pursue value for money in their endeavours (including managing risk appropriately), and act transparently as public entities. The board and management should accept accountability for the proper management of the organisation."[16]

The Code of Practice also provides direction on the formation and management of the board and on regular board meetings. It states that "the preparation and adoption of a strategic plan is a primary responsibility of the Board of a State body" and that "the Board is required to confirm annually ... that the State body has a system of internal financial control in place."

[15] Department of Finance, *Code of Practice for the Governance of State Bodies* (2009).
[16] *Ibid.*

The Code of Practice further discusses codes of conduct, disclosure, ethics, remuneration and risk management. For Irish arts organisations, this list of corporate governance considerations is a good guideline for best practice. All of these considerations are relevant for arts organisations and should at least be addressed by them.

Like the Governance Code, the Code of Practice recognises that an organisation's size will affect the sophistication of its corporate governance systems and that smaller organisations will have more limited resources to spend on corporate governance. Similar to other codes, it recognises that organisational size must determine the level of compliance: "certain requirements of the Code of Practice would have a disproportionate effect on [smaller organisations] because of the nature and scale of their activities".[17]

The Code of Practice does, however, prescribe some disclosure requirements for the annual accounts of state bodies: "Annual reports should also be published on the web-site" and "in the interests of transparency and good governance, State bodies should publish in their Reports details of fees paid to each of their directors, the expenses paid to the Board, broken-down by category, and the salary of the Chief Executive Officer".[18] These stipulations can be considered good practice for publicly funded arts organisations, but they are not consistently adhered to within the arts sector.

Corporate Governance Statements and 'Comply or Explain'

Arts organisations should state in their annual reports that they comply with a particular code of governance and they should explain any non-compliance with that code, using the criteria described below.

Suggested guidelines for a governance statement in an annual report are included in **Appendix 6**. It is good practice for arts organisations to include the following in their annual reports:

- a statement of the governance code that they follow;
- their corporate governance policies, procedures and principles;
- details of the board, its composition and selection policy;
- the number of board meetings held, attendance at the meetings, and any reviews of its own board performance; and
- details of subcommittees and their responsibilities.

---

[17] Department of Finance, *Code of Practice for the Governance of State Bodies* (2009).
[18] *Ibid.*

The corporate governance statement should also discuss the board's strategy and policy on risk management and internal controls.

Arts organisations state in their annual reports whether they comply with certain governance standards or codes. Therefore, they need to explain the instances where they do not comply with certain parts of the selected code or standard. This is widely known as the 'comply or explain' approach.[19] The 'comply or explain' approach has been described as "the trademark of corporate governance in the UK",[20] and the approach is certainly a cornerstone of most governance codes used by Irish arts organisations.

Generally, codes of corporate governance are composed of 'principles' and 'provisions'. The principles are "the core of the Code" and provisions are the ways in which those principles are applied. However, it is recognised that "an alternative to following a provision may be justified in particular circumstances if good governance can be achieved by other means".[21] This means that organisations should comply with the provisions of the code; or, where an alternative to following a provision can be justified, then the reasons should be explained clearly. The organisation should aim to demonstrate how its actual practices are consistent with the *principle* to which the particular provision relates. Furthermore, the organisation should show how non-compliance with a provision "contributes to good governance and promotes delivery of business objectives".[22]

In 2011 an EU green paper, *The EU Corporate Governance Framework*, identified the need to improve the quality of the explanations given in corporate governance statements, contending that "the overall quality of companies' corporate governance statements when departing from a corporate governance code recommendation is unsatisfactory". The paper further stated that "in over 60% of cases where companies chose not to apply recommendations, they did not provide sufficient explanation."[23] They either stated that they had departed from a recommendation without any further

---

[19] The 'comply or explain' approach enjoys the support of regulators both at EU and national levels. The European Commission expressed its preference for this approach by adopting the Directive 2006/46/EC, which mandated the application of corporate governance codes by way of comply or explain. (EU Contract No. ETD/2008/IM/F2/126, 2009, "Study on monitoring and enforcement practices in corporate governance in the member states".)

[20] Financial Reporting Council, *The UK Corporate Governance Code* (2012).

[21] *Ibid.*

[22] *Ibid.*

[23] European Commission, *The EU Corporate Governance Framework*, Green Paper, COM (2011) 164 final.

explanation, or provided only a general or limited explanation.[24] While the green paper only samples listed companies, it is important to remember that better disclosure and transparency leads to better funding opportunities for all organisations.

It is recommended that arts organisations use the 'comply or explain' approach, and that explanations be given for specific non-compliance with whichever code they are using. In its annual report, the organisation should:

- set out the background for the non-compliance with the code, explaining the reasons;
- provide a clear rationale for the action it is taking;
- describe any mitigating actions taken to address additional risk and to maintain compliance with the relevant corporate governance principle; and
- where deviation from a particular provision is intended to be for a limited time or period, the explanation should indicate when the organisation expects to comply with the provision.

In terms of compliance with corporate governance standards, how do organisations measure and evaluate their own corporate governance? They can undergo a corporate governance audit, but where the organisation wishes to self-evaluate or carry out an informal check, some form of dashboard, checklist or evaluation framework is needed. Research conducted for this book found only one such assessment methodology, the SWiFT code, which is discussed below.

The SWiFT Code

For organisations wishing to carry out an assessment of their standards of corporate governance, a simple checklist is useful. The SWiFT ('Standardised Within the Fast Track') Code provides a general assessment, with checklists and questionnaires which allow the evaluation of governance standards.

The primary objective of the SWiFT Code, as stated in "SWiFT 3000",[25] is "to facilitate external assessment of Corporate Governance performance and [it] will also enable companies of varying scale to benchmark their

---

[24] *Ibid.*

[25] National Standards Authority of Ireland, *Code of Practice for Corporate Governance Assessment in Ireland* (2010) NSAI Standards, SWiFT 3000.

performance against these requirements and to provide a standard framework of assessment of compliance with relevant Codes (e.g. OECD Principles of Corporate Governance, the Combined Code on Corporate Governance and the Code of Practice for the Governance of State Bodies)".[26] The SWiFT Code assesses corporate governance based on each of the main principles contained in the *Combined Code* (now updated and renamed the *UK Corporate Governance Code*).

In providing an accessible methodology for carrying out corporate governance assessments, the SWiFT Code is relevant to Irish arts organisations. Furthermore, while an arts organisation may understand corporate governance and may be well governed, an assessment will allow the organisation to show how well governed it is. In terms of transparency to stakeholders and potential funders, such demonstration of good governance in core areas is valuable. Similar to the *UK Corporate Governance Code* and the Governance Code for Community, Voluntary and Charitable Organisations in Ireland, the SWiFT Code identifies core areas for governance. The SWiFT Code recommends the assessment of three core areas:[27]

1. Board composition.
2. Board processes.
3. Execution of the board's role.

Suggested guidelines for reviewing and assessing corporate governance in an arts organisation are included in **Appendix 7**. The methodology is intended for an organisation to carry out its own assessment in preparation for a governance statement in its annual report. Arts organisations differ from non-profit organisations in the assessment of artistic endeavour and the risk involved in producing art. Good governance will take account of that risk, while simultaneously managing it without allowing the organisation to becoming risk averse. This will be done by identifying risks and documenting them at board level, and by setting strategies to mitigate risk and to deal with the fallout of negative outcomes. (Risk management is more fully discussed in **Chapter 7**.)

In the following sections of this chapter, we will discuss aspects and features of the various corporate governance codes so that organisations can decide which elements of governance are relevant for them.

---

[26] *Ibid.*
[27] *Ibid.*

The *Governance Code for Community, Voluntary and Charitable Organisations in Ireland*

The creation of the *Governance Code for Community, Voluntary and Charitable Organisations in Ireland* ('the Governance Code') was prompted by the lack of regulation in the sector and is a useful and accessible document for arts organisations. While not produced for the arts sector specifically, but for the charity sector as a whole, it celebrates being produced "for the sector by the sector", developed as it was by a working group comprised of eight charities.

Insofar as non-profit arts organisations are also charities, the Governance Code is relevant to them. Based on the *UK Corporate Governance Code*, it identifies a "proportionate approach", defining three categories of organisation (Type A, B or C) based on how governance is conducted (see **Table 3.2** below).

Table 3.2   **Organisations Delimited by the Governance Code**

Organisation Categories	Type A Organisation	Type B Organisation	Type C Organisation
Board member's role	Comprehensive, including governance, management and operations.	Primarily governance, but with some management and operational responsibilities	Solely governance, with a clear division between the governance role of the board and the management and operations role of staff.
Staffing	Run by one or more volunteers, who may or may not be board members. Does not employ staff.	Employs one or more full-time/ part-time staff member(s).	Any number of full-time/part-time staff, all reporting to a chief executive/MD.

Source: the *Governance Code for Community, Voluntary and Charitable Organisations in Ireland* (2012).

The Governance Code is based on five main principles, as follows:

1. Leading the organisation
2. Exercising control over the organisation
3. Being transparent and accountable
4. Working effectively
5. Behaving with integrity

These principles are not dissimilar to the principles of the *UK Corporate Governance Code* (i.e. leadership, effectiveness, accountability, remuneration, and relations with shareholders). The similarities between the main codes in operation in Ireland are helpful for organisations in Ireland, as they promote clarity and unity of purpose amongst organisations adopting a governance code.

In addition, the Governance Code specifically states that: "It is expected that groups and organisations will compare themselves to the standards outlined in the Code on a 'comply or explain' basis." It does not make recommendations about accounting disclosures or the identification of standard accounting practices. It does, however, state that adopting the code will:

- reassure funders that donations are being managed by a well-run organisation;
- increase transparency;
- help avoid serious risks;
- help the organisation achieve its goals faster; and
- reduce costs.[28]

Interestingly, the sector identifies a link between good governance and cost reduction, and good governance and transparency.[29] The Governance Code affirms that organisations should adopt it because it is the right thing to do, and that the organisations will benefit in many ways.

The Arts Council Governance Programme

The Arts Council provides active help and guidance to its funded organisations on its website and through its coordinators, sometimes even intervening where there are identifiable problems. The Arts Council's *Code of Governance Framework* (2013) shows how it is governed, and can be found on its

---

[28] The Governance Code (2012), www.governancecode.ie.
[29] The link between good governance and cost reduction and the faster achievement of goals is commonly referred to in the non-profit sector, but no studies have yet proven a causal link.

website, www.artscouncil.ie. It has also produced a guide, "A Practical Guide for Board Members of Arts Organisations", which, for example, states that the common form of legal structure for arts organisations is a company limited by guarantee.[30] It also includes guidance on boards and director's roles.

The Arts Council is accountable for the money it disburses and is a major stakeholder in Irish arts organisations, not just for the stewardship of the money but also for the excellence of the artistic output. Therefore, its guidance is important for those organisations in receipt of or seeking its funding.

Summary

Individual arts organisations face a confusing array of best practices and guidelines for corporate governance. Such organisations need to identify their organisational structure and match it to an appropriate governance code. They may be non-profits, charities or private limited companies, and in each case corporate governance requirements will vary. This chapter has shown that the basic principles are the same regardless of the organisational structure. Organisational size is more likely to determine, on a pragmatic basis, which governance code is best for the arts organisation.

The next chapter addresses the specific concerns of arts organisations in relation to their corporate governance programmes. Arts organisations are different not just because they neither fit into the non-profit nor the for-profit sectors; they have unique issues, conflicts and dynamics. Consideration of corporate governance within arts organisations needs to take account of the difficulty in measuring output and the various methods of defining success.

Corporate governance standards within the arts sector are improving, but from a low base. Currently the non-profit sector has the Governance Code, which applies to all arts organisations classified as non-profit. Although this code does not apply to all arts organisations, it does indicate that the sector is attempting to improve its own governance standards. As we have seen, the Charities Act does not address for arts organisations the need for uniformity of disclosures in financial statements. However, we can look forward to more uniformity in financial reporting when FRS102 is adopted from January 2015. There is much yet to be done, and the conversation concerning transparency of financial information in arts organisations has not yet started. Therefore, stakeholders (who are also us, the taxpayers) can still reasonably ask: "Where has the money gone?" The next chapter will start to address this concern.

---

[30] The Arts Council, "A Practical Guide for Board Members of Arts Organisations" (2006).

Chapter 4

Compliance and Measurement: Considerations for Directors

The measures of success or failure are expressed in terms of quality of work, standards achieved, benefits to the community, quality of life enhanced for audiences, pride in success.
Phelim Donlon, *Governance in Arts Organisations in Ireland* (2005)

Introduction

Having discussed the concerns of individual arts organisations regarding standards of corporate governance, this chapter now seeks to answer the question: "So, where do we start?" In answering this question, we will identify areas where arts organisations, by their nature and composition, are at risk of non-compliance, examining compliance issues and problems that are peculiar to such organisations and their possible resolutions.

Finally, in researching this book, arts organisations expressed to me a range of difficulties they have with governance. This chapter offers guidance for compliance with governance standards and a roadmap for implementing governance programmes.

If you want to improve corporate governance, the best place to start is with the board of directors. Governance should flow from the board. We have seen that arts organisations can fall into a number of categories of corporate entity and that it is possible to associate best corporate governance practices with the various types. The board should select the governance code and framework that best applies to their organisation and work to comply with those requirements. (For more on the role of the board, see **Chapter 5**.)

Compliance with a governance code means complying with the obligations set out by that code. It will then be possible to state that the organisation is 'compliant' and stating compliance allows readers of the annual report to have reassurance and visibility on how the organisation is being run and how the directors are governing, controlling and directing.

The Irish non-profit sector has been under-regulated,[1] and most Irish arts organisations would fall into the same (under-regulated) category. Despite the key pieces of legislation discussed in the preceding chapters, the establishment of a Charities Regulatory Authority was only recently announced after six years of calls from the sector for a regulator.[2] The Authority was set up in 2014. Currently, the sector regulates itself and standards of compliance have therefore rested within the sector.

There is a concern that arts organisations can be non-compliant through ignorance or lack of information. Additionally, codes and best practices are not fully promulgated throughout the sector.[3] This is no excuse for non-compliance, however, and it is a worry for many arts boards. However, embedding corporate governance standards and measuring outcomes is particularly relevant for arts organisations because they do not readily measure outcomes in terms of profitability; their performance is more often gauged by grant receipts, footfall, attendances and other relevant measures.

Many of the arts organisations I have worked with express the same concerns about compliance with governance standards and best practices. They fear that they may be non-compliant and need to act quickly. However, at the same time, they do not want to spend too much money or time on what they do not deem part of their core purpose. Therefore, they need to choose governance programmes that can be easily implemented and communicated. The best way to do this is to openly identify and address the problems rather than hiding them, or indeed hiding from them.

Embedding Corporate Governance

In a typical arts organisation, few people may be directly involved in governance and related issues. Consequently, corporate governance issues may be left to the board and largely ignored by the organisation as a whole. In such cases, the board will need to work with the CEO and act to embed the principles of good governance throughout the organisation. There are some basic principles that will help the board to do this; some of these are governance-related and some relate to internal controls. Without internal controls,

---

[1] Dóchas, "A Dóchas Briefing Charities Regulation & Legislation" (March 2006).

[2] Holland, K., "New Authority to Regulate Charities", *The Irish Times*, 10 July 2013.

[3] In a recent survey of non-profits in Ireland, 40% stated that they "were not aware of any code of governance". (Grant Thornton Not-for-Profit Survey 2012)

governance will not be effective because the organisation will struggle to produce measures of performance upon which the board can rely when making decisions. Basic principles and measures to implement include:

- The mission statement and/or strategy document for the organisation should be communicated throughout the organisation and acted upon. A measure of success is when everyone knows the organisation's primary objective and that the achievement of that objective is part of their responsibility.
- The directors need to ensure that internal controls are operational and effective. A management letter is usually issued by the auditors after the year-end audit, which addresses any deficiencies in internal controls and makes recommendations on how to resolve them.
- The board will need to periodically approve budgets and forecasts, review management accounts and compare interim outcomes of the approved budget. And review may not always be sufficient; the board may need to charge the executives with resolving budgetary deficits, implementing cost cuts or changing strategic plans in order to avoid cash shortages or financial losses.

Some basic internal controls need to be in place to ensure that the reports issued to the board are adequate for decision making. Fundamental internal controls include controls over expenditure, cash and bank accounts. For organisations of any size, tiers of cheque-signing and fund-transfer authorities are desirable. For example, there should be at least two nominated signatories for cheques up to a certain amount. Beyond that amount, at least one of the signatories should be the chief executive. For decisions that require board approval, that approval should be attached to the cheque requests. In this way there will be a strict hierarchy of people enabled to commit the organisation to expenditure that would be material for the organisation.

Protection of employees is also at stake. The existence of procedures around cash and cheques helps protect employees from mistakes or misappropriation by others. The protection of an organisation's employees helps to ensure the sustainability of that organisation.

Measuring Success?

Good governance suggests that arts organisations do not just operate within their financial budgets but also measure the outcomes of their artistic programmes against their mission and vision statements. Mission and vision statements for arts organisations are aspirational and in many cases are declarations of artistic purpose.

The Abbey Theatre, Ireland's national theatre, provides its mission statement on its website:

> "The Abbey Theatre was founded as Ireland's national theatre, by W.B. Yeats and Lady Gregory in 1904, to bring upon the stage the deeper emotions of Ireland. Although written more than a hundred years ago, this is still the kernel of what constitutes the artistic imperative for the Abbey Theatre today."[4]

The difficulty in measuring or making tangible the artistic imperative of staging our "deeper emotions" needs no elaboration.

The mission statement of the Irish Museum of Modern Art (IMMA) also features prominently on its website:

> "The Museum's mission is to foster within society an awareness, understanding and involvement in the visual arts through policies and programmes which are excellent, innovative and inclusive."[5]

We may agree that IMMA has achieved "excellence" and has fostered "awareness", but satisfactorily *proving* this will elude even the most practiced performance measurers.

The question of how to measure the success of an arts organisation is fundamental. Would, for example, measuring the footfall to IMMA in a year be a good measure of the "inclusiveness" it wants to achieve? And can footfall measure the quality of the artistic output? Should we measure media coverage, or accolades from peer organisations? None of these criteria fully measures success, showing how difficult it is to judge such things in arts organisations. Moreover, innovative art, music and drama are not necessarily popular and so artistic curators are known to judge themselves by public outcry as a measure of achievement; sometimes greatness in art is vilified when it appears before its time.[6]

---

[4] www.abbeytheatre.ie/about (accessed November 2013).

[5] www.imma.ie (accessed November 2013).

[6] In 1926, W.B. Yeats famously declared to rioters in the Abbey Theatre, in reference to the riots after Sean O'Casey's *The Plough and the Stars*: "You have disgraced yourselves again; is this to be the recurring celebration of the arrival of Irish genius?" (Yeats said "again" in reference to riots following the 1907 premiere of J.M. Synge's controversial *Playboy of the Western World*. Both plays are now celebrated as Irish classics.)

In his report, *Capturing Cultural Value*, John Holden addresses the issues of cultural organisations "setting their activities against formal objectives, and seeking to justify activity and expenditure against 'outcomes."[7] Holden notes:

"A growing sense of unease pervades the cultural sector as it sets about justifying its consumption of public money. Instead of talking about what they do – displaying pictures or putting on dance performances – organisations will need to demonstrate how they have contributed to wider policy agendas, such as social inclusion, crime prevention and learning. The problem is particularly acute in the relationship between local authorities and the cultural organisations that they fund. Even where targets refer to cultural activities, they are often expressed in terms of efficiency, cost-per-user and audience diversity, rather than discussed in terms of cultural achievement."[8]

An Arts Council publication by journalist Emer O'Kelly advances a similar argument against equating commercial success with quality in art:

"They are both skewed, and prove just how far outside our core values artistic appreciation is. And this will continue as long as we scrabble to impose an 'artistic module' from the outside, chasing arts ratings by following rather than leading public understanding and taste, and all the time under-estimating public appetite and understanding."[9]

O'Kelly discusses the dynamic of providing funding to arts organisations and expecting to be able to prove that it has been used successfully. Rather than resisting measurement entirely, Holden and O'Kelly highlight the dangers of measurement, showing how current measurement practices can interfere with and even compromise artistic output.

Questions then arise about whether we want to measure our cultural institutions. What is the fairest measurement? Will measurement itself curtail these organisations and impact artistic outcomes? We are left with the question we asked at the beginning: What will we measure? Funders of the arts are concerned about corporate governance, but their focus is more on stewardship of monies rather than evaluating or judging artistic outcomes. For arts organisations, the proper and transparent accounting for all monies, together with adequate internal controls, goes a long way toward satisfying

---

[7] Holden, J., *Capturing Cultural Value: How culture has become a tool of government policy* (Demos, 2004).

[8] *Ibid.*

[9] O'Kelly, E., *The Case for Elitism* (The Arts Council, 2007).

the interests of funders. Inevitably, however, measures of success will need to be used: attracting funders and donors in the first instance involves demonstrating the quality and merit of planned artistic activities. This process inherently involves one arts organisation attempting to prove that it is of greater merit than another organisation competing for the same funding.

Arts organisations may define themselves by their artistic merit, values and aims, but these values and aims can neither be heard nor appreciated without the strategic alignment of corporate governance in creating fundable organisations that provide good value for stakeholders' money. (Valuation and measurement is further discussed in **Chapter 6**.)

Accountability and the Use of Websites

Accountability is an important element in the process of showing and proving that an arts organisation merits funding. It is the expectation that an organisation's management is ultimately responsible for acting in the best interests of external stakeholders, for example funders and audience. The idea that funded organisations are accountable to the public is unanimous among the funders surveyed for this book.

An organisation's website is a primary source of interaction with stakeholders, so it needs to be accessible, transparent and user-friendly. Funders are reassured by the timely availability of current financial statements on the arts organisation's website. The financial statements should be comprehensive and endeavour to show more, rather than less information. The onus is on the organisation to prove accountability and show that stakeholders' funds are being used for the purposes for which they are given.

Websites are also a way of presenting, and for the organisation *remembering*, vision and mission statements (as in the Abbey Theatre and IMMA examples above). The website should also be used to show alignment of vision and mission with financial accountability. Good governance demands that the vision and mission be aligned with the organisation's financial disclosures and the 'story' told in the annual report. For example, an annual report which shows that the organisation is being run at a loss but declares a mission statement of running the organisation within its budgets is demonstrating a lack of alignment; the annual report and the mission statement both lose credibility. Similarly, any images, graphs or photographs in the annual report should tell the same story as the financial statements and should be aligned to the mission statement.

Arts Organisations as Public Benefit Entities

The European Union Recommendations 2008[10] uses the phrase "Public Interest Entities" to define entities which are loosely defined in Ireland as 'non-profits'. The Financial Reporting Standards Board defines a "public benefit entity" (PBE) as:

> "An entity whose primary objective is to provide goods or services for the general public, community or social benefit and where any equity is provided with a view to supporting the entity's primary objectives rather than with a view to providing a financial return to equity providers, shareholders or members."[11]

From a governance perspective, such terms, definitions and the thinking behind them should encourage arts organisations to confidently position their primary objectives in benefitting society as part of their organisational strategies. Arts organisations are no longer simply 'non-profits' or 'not-for-profits' (does this imply they are *for-losses*?). Implied in use of the term 'non-profit' for a cultural organisation is a financial evaluation. And it is arguable that arts organisations need to be judged on their values and output rather than on profits or breakeven financial results. The success of the organisation in achieving its primary objective (artistic output based on the organisation's values), rather than merely its financial returns, should be central to its governance structure. In "supporting the entity's primary objectives",[12] good corporate governance enables the achievement of artistic objectives.

Board Members and Conflicts of Interest

Achieving objectives and measuring success is dependent on a functioning board. In the following sections and into the next chapter, we will discuss some of the more common issues experienced with boards that are of particular relevance to arts organisations.

---

[10] "Co-operation between Member States is a priority with regard to audits of public interest entities" (Commission Recommendation of 6 May 2008 on external quality assurance for statutory auditors and audit firms auditing public interest entities (notified under document number C(2008) 1721) (2008/362/EC)).

[11] Accounting Standards Board, "Financial Reporting Standard for Public Benefit Entities and Consequential Amendments to Proposals in FRED 44 Financial Reporting Standard for Small and Medium-sized Entities", Exposure Draft, Number 45 (London 2011), p. 17.

[12] *Ibid.*

Good governance requires directors to be independent and to act in the best interests of the organisation. However, many arts organisations experience board dysfunction where some members are representatives of other, related organisations, often causing conflicts of interest for the director/board member involved. If a board member is required to make a decision that affects both of the organisations on whose boards he or she serves, a conflict of interest can arise. While the Companies Acts require directors to act in the best interests of the company, this becomes difficult if the board member is serving two related organisations. For example, this can occur where a board member is also a director or employee of another organisation that is being funded. The board member is then a giver of funds on the funder organisation, and a receiver of the same funds in the organisation being funded. It would seem impossible in this situation for the person who is involved with both organisations to make an objective decision.

It is common for arts organisations to have representatives on their board from their largest sponsors or donors. Indeed, funders often include a clause in the funding agreement that entitles them to a place or places on the board. This can lead to a person being appointed a director of the board as a representative of the funder, seeing themselves as representing the interests of the funder. This is not good governance. Well-governed organisations have independent directors, aware of their statutory duty to act in the best interests of the company, and not in their own interests or those of another organisation. Directors have a duty to avoid conflicts of interests, and representing one organisation on the board of another organisation creates a conflict of interest. This is a difficult issue; small arts organisations may welcome the expertise of their funder on the board. Additionally, the funder may perceive difficulty at board level and may want to act to resolve it in person to ensure the sustainability of the organisation and the safety and effectiveness of their funds.

Boards should have a clear and comprehensive policy on conflicts of interest, and this should be distributed to all board members. However, when a board member is effectively a representative for a funder, there is no clear solution. One partially effective solution is for funders to have the right to sit on the board as an observer and advisor. Another solution is for the arts organisation to have a standing offer of advice from the funder, again should advice be needed. However, it is advisable for the funder to exit the board when the problem is resolved to allow the independent directors to lead the company.

Board Effectiveness and the Artistic Director

When arts organisations refer to 'directors', rather than members of the board, they often mean those who provide artistic direction. The artistic director of a theatre or gallery is a key driver of organisational goals and indeed of artistic excellence. This confusion for performing arts organisations is described by Phelim Donlon:

> "In performing arts organisations, the title 'Director' can often be confusing. It may mean a member of the board. It may mean the Chief Executive, or it may mean the person who has directed the production. So, a figure against 'Directors' in the accounts of a performing arts organisation will almost always mean fees paid to persons to direct productions, rather than fees paid to members of the Board or to the Chief Executive."[13]

If the arts organisation is a company limited by guarantee and is a registered charity, it must comply with the Companies Acts as well as the Charities Acts,[14] which prohibit paying directors for holding the office of director. Furthermore, the Revenue Commissioners' guidelines on charities state: "Directors/Trustees are not to be paid for holding such an office". Thus, a charitable organisation cannot remunerate its directors and therefore cannot have beneficiaries as directors on the board.[15] For many arts organisations, this means that the artistic director cannot be a board member. Yet the artistic director directs the artistic programme and is responsible for the artistic output of the organisation, which is its primary objective. Many arts organisations naturally appoint the artistic director to the board, but where the artistic director is being paid by the charity, the director cannot be a trustee or statutory director. This often leads to confusion: first that the artistic 'director' is not a statutory director, and secondly that the artistic director cannot sit on the board and vote. A solution (though not a perfect one) is to get unpaid directors who are artists to sit on the board, or to invite the artistic director to attend board meetings as an officer of the company, but without any voting rights, or rights as a board member.

---

[13] Donlon, P., "Governance in Arts Organisations in Ireland" (2005) in *Practitioner Perspectives on Nonprofit Governance*, Centre for Nonprofit Management, School of Business, Trinity College Dublin.

[14] There are three main charities acts in Ireland: the Charities Act 1961, the Charities Act 1973, and the Charities Act 2009.

[15] In general, no payments should be paid to directors/trustees other than out-of-pocket expenses.

Shadow Directors

It is important for arts organisations that are incorporated to be aware that when they have significant and active stakeholders who can exercise control on the board, they may need to consider the risk that those who have that type of controlling influence could be deemed 'shadow directors' under company law. Shadow directors are typically those who exercise control and power in the organisation, but are not listed as directors. For example, funders who assist the company or who are involved in implementing the terms of the funding agreement could, in certain circumstances, be considered shadow directors. A shadow directorship can be deemed to exist even if the director has not been formally appointed as such. The main implications of a person being deemed a shadow director is that he or she is subject to the same duties and obligations as duly appointed directors of the board. As stated in section 27 of the Companies Act 1990:

> "…a person in accordance with whose directions or instructions the directors of a company are accustomed to act (in this Act referred to as '*a shadow director*') shall be treated for the purposes of this Part as a director of the company unless the directors are accustomed so to act by reason only that they do so on advice given by him in a professional capacity."

The Companies Acts grant that shadow directors are not guilty of an offence simply by being shadow directors. However, if issues arise and problems occur and, for example, the directors are accused of reckless trading, any shadow directors will be treated as directors of the company and also accused of reckless trading. On the other side of this equation, if a contract is entered into by the board but a shadow director was not involved in the decision, the shadow director can claim an infringement of his or her rights as a director. A shadow director may also be the subject of a restriction or disqualification order by the Office of the Director of Corporate Enforcement (ODCE).

For arts organisations that are limited companies, the test of whether a stakeholder is a shadow director is to ask whether such a person exerts such an influence over the company's directors that those directors are accustomed to acting according to that person's instructions. The shadow director, then, has many of the legal responsibilities of a director. Ignorance is not an excuse, and being unaware of the existence of the shadow directorship releases neither the shadow director nor the company from its duties relating to the directorship.

Directors' Liabilities and Responsibilities in Difficult Times

Directors have a duty of care to the company they serve. This means that they must act in the best interests of that company. In difficult financial circumstances, this can involve taking measures to keep the company solvent, such as close scrutiny of the company's financial affairs, cost-cutting, debt negotiation and/or the direction or organisation of additional fundraising activities. (A factsheet for directors, outlining their duties, responsibilities and liabilities during financial uncertainty, is reproduced in **Appendix 2**, and the Arts Council's "Practical Guide for Board Members of Arts Organisations" is also helpful in this regard.)[16]

Directors' duties include:

- taking reasonable steps to ensure proper books of account are kept, and that an annual audit is carried out; and
- ensuring that annual returns are made to the Companies Registration Office.

There are a number of steps directors should take to improve the organisation's financial circumstances and so that they can defend themselves against possible charges of reckless trading:

- Convene more frequent board meetings, and encourage frequent meetings of the executive management team. Call an extraordinary general meeting (EGM) of members if necessary.
- Take careful minutes and record decisions taken, noting the reasons and bases for these decisions as well as relevant dates and deadlines. Ensure the minutes are complete and accurate and are securely filed.
- Obtain financial advice, preferably from a qualified accountant.
- Prepare, or have prepared, regular management accounts to get a realistic picture of the organisation's state of affairs.
- Prepare a budget and a realistic business plan.
- Hold early discussions with the bank and keep them informed.
- For the largest creditors, keep them informed of your plans and, if necessary, negotiate payment plans with them. Only make promises that can be kept.
- If the organisation is insolvent, get insolvency advice from an insolvency practitioner or a qualified accountant.
- Discuss the situation with the organisation's auditors.

---

[16] The Arts Council, "A Practical Guide for Board Members of Arts Organisations" (2006).

The Companies Bill 2012 states directors' duties comprehensively, and directors will be required to include a 'compliance statement' in their directors' reports.

Rights and Duties of the Members of a Company

For all arts organisations that are incorporated (as either a limited company or one limited by guarantee), when organising the annual general meeting (AGM) of any limited company, the directors and the company secretary often need to distinguish between 'members' of the company and 'members' who pay a subscription to a representative organisation. The Companies Acts define the members of a company as the "subscribers to the Memorandum of Association and such other persons as the directors shall admit to membership".[17] When a company is set up, the members are listed on the Memorandum and Articles of Association. In standard Memorandums and Articles, such members are required to be invited to general meetings of the company.

Many arts organisations have members who pay an annual subscription (arts resource organisations are a good example). These members are not necessarily the statutory members or subscribers of the company; in some cases they more closely resemble customers for the services supplied by the arts organisation.

This distinction is not often made and sometimes arts organisations invite their annual subscription members to their AGMs; however, they must also invite their statutory members (i.e. "subscribers" as identified above). The company may also discover that its general meetings are not properly convened if all of the statutory members have not been invited. It is therefore important to make the distinction between statutory members and annual subscription payers or customers. Sometimes these groups are different; when these groups are not different, the register of members should include the subscribers to the Memorandum and Articles *and* the annual subscription-paying members.

The *members* of a company, and therefore the members of arts organisations that are incorporated, are defined in the Companies Acts:

> "The subscribers of a company are the members, and those whose names are on the company's register of members are the members of the company. The subscribers of the memorandum of a company shall be deemed to have

---

[17] Companies Act 1963, Table C.

agreed to become members of the company and, on its registration, shall be entered as members in its register of members. Every other person who agrees to become a member of a company, and whose name is entered in its register of members, shall be a member of the company."

The members have certain rights and duties. For instance, the members:

- appoint the board at the annual general meeting of the company;
- appoint the auditors;
- approve the accounts and vote on any changes to the Memorandum and Articles; and
- can wind up or liquidate the company (as in a 'members' voluntary liquidation').

The Companies Acts also stipulate that every company must keep a register of its members and the following particulars:

"(a) the names, addresses of the members, and, in the case of a company having a share capital, a statement of the shares held by each member, distinguishing each share by its number so long as the share has a number, and of the amount paid or agreed to be considered as paid on the shares of each member;

(b) the date at which each person was entered in the register as a member; and

(c) the date at which any person ceased to be a member."[18]

Directors of the company become members only if their names are entered on the register of members, and they cease to become members when they notify the company in writing. For arts organisations, the register of members defines the list of who needs to be notified of and invited to the AGM; therefore, it is advisable to keep the number of members up to date and to be clear on who the members are.

Winding Up

From time to time arts organisations need to 'wind up' or cease operations. There are aspects of compliance in relation to winding up that are often not considered until an organisation is at a late stage of the process. Some basic considerations are outlined here and also detailed in **Appendix 2**.

---

[18] Companies Act 1963, section 116.

There are various ways of winding up a company. One common way is a members' voluntary liquidation. This is a form of winding up whereby the members decide, for commercial reasons, to wind up the company.

For arts organisations that are companies limited by guarantee with or without charitable status, there is a restriction on how funds are distributed on a winding up of the company. A special provision limiting how distributions of any surpluses are made on a winding up is usually inserted into the Memorandum and Articles governing the company. An example of such a clause is as follows:

> "If upon the winding up or dissolution of the Company there remains after the satisfaction of all its debts and liabilities, any property whatsoever, the same shall not be paid to or distributed among the members of the Company but shall be given or transferred to some other charitable institution or institutions having main objects similar to the main object(s) of the Company..."

This clause is from a standard Memorandum and Articles of Association for a company limited by guarantee and seeking tax exemption as a charity under the provisions of section 207 of the Taxes Consolidation Act 1997, produced by the Revenue Commissioners (the Revenue grants charitable status to organisations).

Summary

Compliance with corporate governance standards is no more difficult for arts organisation than for other organisations; it simply has its own peculiarities. Compliance is important for all organisations, and finding the best framework and programme to ensure clear and simple compliance is a fundamental step. When corporate governance standards are in place, arts organisations may wish to evaluate these programmes. However, due to the nature of arts organisations, many being public benefit entities, this evaluation needs to consider some unique elements.

Arts organisations are different: their output and success is usually difficult to measure objectively. An Arts Council study of audiences interestingly notes: "the public ... consider the arts to be important, even if they do not personally attend at formal arts events".[19] A strange conundrum exists: a society is greatly enriched by great art and that society often judges itself

[19] McAuliffe, J., "The Siren Alps", *The Value of the Arts* (The Arts Council, 2007).

by the quality of its artistic output, but how do we know that the art we fund is excellent if we do not participate in its appreciation?

There are difficulties in measuring artistic outcomes, and in a dynamic way the measurement itself can impair the artistic output. However, it is possible to measure the success of an organisation's compliance with good governance standards, and this compliance is a measure of suitability for future funding.

The output of governance programmes is determined by the direction of the board and its ability to lead and to maintain a good governance program. The mix in composition and operation of the board of directors will be discussed next as a cornerstone of good governance.

Chapter 5

The Board of Directors

Nobody is supposed to know everything

A quote from "Walking with The Comrades".
An intentional Naxalite tactic.
An unfortunate reality.
A helpful reminder.
A calming mantra.

Julia Reichard (2012)

Introduction

Corporate governance comes from the board, which sets the standards of governance for the organisation. As a group, therefore, the board of directors needs to have the collective experience and knowledge to do this. The board should have diverse knowledge and skills: interviewees and clients have emphasised the need for financial, governance, legal and communications skills as well as the relevant artistic skills for boards. The board's direction should ensure compliance not just with statutory requirements but with best practice in corporate governance.

While nobody is supposed to know everything, a well-run board with diverse skills, clear objectives and good governance standards will produce better results as a whole board acting together rather than as a fragmented or indifferent board. A well-run board may even be an enabler for great art.

Arts organisations can encounter difficulties with boards, for example with the recruitment of board members, clarity around their roles, replacement and succession planning, and the handling of conflicts of interest. These and other problems will be discussed in this chapter in the context of a well-functioning board of directors.

The Role of the Board of Directors

In addition to corporate governance, the alignment of strategy with operations and artistic direction should also come from the board. Corporate governance is an important and pivotal role for the board of directors in any arts organisation. In terms of major grant-givers, the Arts Council considers the importance of the role of the board in its "A Practical Guide for Board Members of Arts Organisations", which holds that "the board interprets and guards the mission of the organisation" and "the board establishes policy".[1] Arts organisations in Ireland are already generally aware of the importance of the boards, the experience and diversity of its members, and how it should set strategy and organisational values.

The increasing importance of the role of the board is further highlighted in the European Commission's 2011 green paper, *The EU Corporate Governance Framework*, which identifies the need for diversity on boards, recommending professional, international and gender diversity.[2]

The boards of many Irish arts organisations are comprised of voluntary positions. These boards therefore differ from the paid board positions of many for-profit organisations. While the boards of arts organisations can be more hands-on, involved and passionate about the values the organisation brings to the community or society, because these positions are often voluntary and unpaid, board members may not be able to afford to devote the necessary time to the organisation. Yet the duties of statutory directors are the same for paid board positions as for non-paid, and the expected contributions are the same.

The cornerstones of a well-run board include:

- monthly/bi-monthly meetings with agendas, minutes and actions;
- monthly/quarterly financial reporting in the organisation, which is presented at board meetings;
- good alignment of the executive management team and the board, with a proactive approach to problems and issues, and no defensiveness to any questions;
- a transparent appointment process for electing independent board members;
- an effective and independent chairperson;

---

[1] The Arts Council, "A Practical Guide for Board Members of Arts Organisations" (2006).
[2] European Commission, *The EU Corporate Governance Framework*, Green Paper, COM (2011) 164 final.

- a decision-making process that is clear and understood by all the attendees of board meetings;
- a finance committee with a chairperson who is independent of the operation of the company;
- an active Company Secretary who understands and can apply the relevant provisions of the Companies Acts.

For the arts organisations I have interviewed or worked with directly, while such basic principles are often accepted, they can be difficult to achieve and to maintain.

Board and Organisational Values

Boards work best where members share a common set of values, the values of the organisation, which in turn determine its culture. Some interviewees indicated that they look at the values of the organisation and its board before they accept a board position. On the subject of harmonised values with the stakeholders, Paul Dunn notes that "incongruence occurs when values and activities of a nonprofit are inconsistent with the values and activities of a donor".[3] Further comments on values are made by the Arts Council and the Financial Reporting Council: good governance should align these values by "demonstrating integrity"[4] and "aligning strategy".[5]

It is often evident to observers when the board and the organisation and/or the stakeholders are at odds with each other, or when values are not correlated. Symptoms include a lack of clarity on objectives, poor business decision-making, poor artistic quality, budget overruns, etc. Interviewees from the Irish arts sector cited a number of examples of organisational problems stemming from the board; one funder observed that when problems arise, "the best place to start [to identify the problems] is with the board".

---

[3] Dunn, P., "Strategic Responses by a Nonprofit when a Donor becomes Tainted" (2010) Vol. 39, No. 1, *Nonprofit and Voluntary Sector Quarterly*, 102–23.
[4] The Arts Council, "Assessment of the Economic Impact of the Arts in Ireland" (November 2011) Arts and Culture Scoping Research Project by Indecon International Economic Consultants.
[5] Financial Reporting Council, *The UK Corporate Governance Code* (2010).

A Well-balanced Board

The *UK Corporate Governance Code* states: "There should be a formal, rigorous and transparent procedure for the appointment of new directors to the board." In previous versions of the Code, in 2010 and 2012, a supporting principle recognising the value of diversity in the boardroom was included after the main principle, which stated: "The search for board candidates should be conducted, and appointments made, on merit, against objective criteria and with due regard for the benefits of diversity on the board, including gender".[6]

During the research for this book, professionals involved in arts organisations invariably raised the importance of diversity on boards and it is now widely recognised that a board will be more effective in directing an organisation when it contains a wide diversity of skills and representative views. For example, boards that consist mainly of artists or musicians have been shown to be less effective than boards where diverse experience, skills and disciplines are deliberately represented. The EU green paper on corporate governance,[7] published in April 2011, provides guidance on the composition of boards and board diversity, which is pertinent to arts organisations: "Diversity in the members' profiles and backgrounds gives the board a range of values, views and sets of competencies."[8] It recommends professional, international and gender diversity as optimal for the composition of a good board.

Smaller organisations in the cultural sector are likely to have smaller boards, usually made up of people who have a professional interest in the particular arts discipline, for example music or dance. My research shows that arts organisations are also aware of specific competencies required by their boards. For example, most small arts organisations tend to have an accountant and/or a solicitor on their boards, professional skills and knowledge that will help guide the organisation through financial, legal compliance and governance issues.

While it is beneficial for board members to have a particular interest or expertise in the activities of the organisation on whose board they sit, there is a risk that the board may have the right artistic skills but not the right technical and governance skills. The appropriate mix of board member skills can

---

[6] Financial Reporting Council, *The UK Corporate Governance Code* (2010); Financial Reporting Council (2012)

[7] European Commission, *The EU Corporate Governance Framework*, Green Paper, COM (2011) 164 final.

[8] *Ibid.*

be achieved in the recruitment process. For instance, Boardmatch Ireland, which pairs organisations with board members through its information and awareness programme, is beneficial to organisations in the arts sector in this regard.[9] The work of Boardmatch Ireland and similar initiatives is important for the arts sector to ensure a pool of suitable candidates for its boards.

Ultimately, it is the *range* of skills and values that is so important for a well-functioning board. Diversity among members gives the board a breadth of values and viewpoints, as well as professional skills.

Selecting Board Members

The 2014 scandal involving the selection of a member of the board of the Irish Museum of Modern Art without adequate consultation with the existing board and without the candidate having the prerequisite skills caused consternation and emphasised the need for a fair and transparent selection process. Writing in *The Irish Times*, Fintan O'Toole asked, "Does the appointment of McNulty to board of Imma meet the seven principles of public office?"[10] Writing on the same matter in the *Irish Examiner*, Gerard Howlin argued that, "There should be no impulse by State to suffocate artistic freedom".[11]

Being fair and transparent in selecting members is a challenge for any board, yet the selection of board members tends not to be addressed in many discussions on corporate governance, as it is difficult to frame a set of rules to follow. The selection process is vital to the recruitment of effective board members; in many cases funders and grant-givers will have a keen interest in who is on the board. Organisations need to be careful that their board selection process is transparent, to avoid accusations of creating a group of 'friends of the chairman' or an 'old boys' club'. At the same time, however, no prospective board member wants to offer his or her services and ultimately be rejected by the board. There is a delicate balance in having a fair and transparent selection process and being respectful of candidates (who are often voluntary and who may not wish for their names to be disclosed if they risk being unsuccessful). The guiding principle is that the recruitment of board members should be about serving the needs of the

---

[9] www.boardmatch.ie (accessed 20 July 2011).

[10] O'Toole, F., "Does the appointment of McNulty to board of Imma meet the seven principles of public office?" *The Irish Times*, 30 September 2014.

[11] Howlin, G., "There should be no impulse by State to suffocate artistic freedom", *Irish Examiner*, 1 October 2014.

board as a collective group. (An example of a policy and procedure for recruiting new board members is provided in **Appendix 1**.)

The basis of a good recruitment policy includes a 'needs analysis', which should be carried out by the whole board to identify what additional skills it needs or the skills gaps that will be left by departing board members. Once identified, such skills gaps should be filled by incoming board members, and the organisation will need to actively seek out candidates with those skills. If, for example, the analysis finds that accountancy skills are needed on the board, it will then be reasonable to advertise or to approach suitable candidates. In this way, the search can be focused and efficient, and the process need not take an unreasonable amount of time.

Gender Diversity on Boards

Arts organisations are often more concerned with professional diversity on their boards than with gender diversity (although gender diversity is better in arts organisations than in other sectors). This is particularly true of small and medium-sized arts organisations because there is a need for a diversity of professional skills on their boards to complement those of relatively small management teams. However, a significant, positive impact can also be made on a board by seeking gender diversity. The European Commission green paper, *The EU Corporate Governance Framework*, states that:

> "Gender diversity can contribute to tackling groupthink. There is also evidence that women have different leadership styles, attend more board meetings and have a positive impact on the collective intelligence of a group. Studies suggest there is a positive correlation between the percentage of women in boards and corporate performance."[12]

Interestingly, a European Commission progress report from 2012 argues that: "A gender-balanced board is more likely to pay attention to managing and controlling risk."[13] Organisations with high inherent risk could perhaps benefit from implementing a better gender balance on their boards, or to identify female values and male values in their decision-making processes and bring each to bear more consciously on their riskier decisions.

---

[12] European Commission, *The EU Corporate Governance Framework*, Green Paper, COM (2011) 164 final, p. 7.
[13] European Commission, *Women in economic decision-making in the EU: Progress report* (2012).

The European Commission's database on women and men in decision-making shows[14] that the share of women on the boards of the largest publicly listed companies in Ireland for 2010–2012 was a mere 8.7%.[15] While no official statistics exist for Irish arts organisations, a review (see **Table 5.1** below) of the websites of nine large Irish arts organisations shows that an average ratio of 35% of board members are women. Compared to the

Table 5.1   **A Short Website Survey of the Percentage of Women on the Boards of Major Irish Arts Organisations**

Arts Organisation	Total Board Members	No. of Women on the Board	Data Source	%	Comments
NCH	15	8	2014 website	53.3%	
IMMA	9	4	2014 website	44.4%	
Abbey Theatre	11	4	2014 website	36.3%	
Gate Theatre	6	2	2014 website	33.3%	
Wexford Opera House	12	2	2014 website	16.67%	
National Gallery	15	6	2014 website	40%	Includes *ex officio* members.
Crawford Gallery	15	6	2014 website	40%	Based on 2011 most recent annual report on website.
Glucksmann Gallery	8	3	2014 website	37.5%	
Arts Council	13	7	2014 website	53.8%	
Totals and Average	104	42		**40.38%**	

Sources: organisational websites (accessed in September 2014).

[14] See http://ec.europa.eu/justice/gender-equality/gender-decision-making/database/index_en.htm.
[15] The table of these findings is reproduced in **Appendix 4**.

national average for our largest companies of 8.7%, Irish arts organisations display much better gender diversity than average organisations.

In May 2010, the Financial Reporting Council (FRC) revised the *Combined Code* to include, for the first time, a principle recognising the value of diversity in the boardroom, stating that "the search for board candidates should be conducted, and appointments made, on merit, against objective criteria and with due regard for the benefits of diversity on the board, including gender".[16] In October 2011 the FRC announced its decision to amend the *Combined Code* to strengthen the principle on boardroom diversity.

According to the European Commission's progress report cited above:

> "The EU cannot afford to permit systematic gender imbalance at the top level of economic decision-making any longer. Gender diversity on boards contributes to improving corporate governance and companies with a higher share of women in senior decision-making positions have been shown to consistently outperform their competitors without that asset."[17]

The Vice President of the European Commission and EU Commissioner for Justice, Fundamental Rights and Citizenship, Viviane Reding, has asked all publicly listed companies to pledge to have at least 30% female board members by 2015 and 40% by 2020. While Irish arts organisations appear to be better than their for-profit counterparts in terms of gender diversity on their boards, some will be challenged to comply with the goal of having 40% women on boards of directors by 2020.

Thus, initiatives to improve gender diversity are important to our arts organisations and can be expected to improve governance. A Credit Suisse report has found that: "There is unusually strong consensus within academic research that a greater number of women on the board improves performance on corporate governance metrics."[18] For Irish arts organisations that are concerned with corporate governance and wish to improve their performance in this area, one simple solution is to put more women on the board.

---

[16] The *Combined Code* cited in Sealy, R. *et al.*, *Women on Boards: 6 Months Monitoring Report* Cranfield University School of Management (October 2011).

[17] European Commission, *Women in economic decision-making in the EU: Progress report* (2012).

[18] Credit Suisse, *Gender diversity and corporate performance* (2012).

Succession Planning

Part of the board's role is to ensure its own successful continuance and any board will need to address the issue of succession planning. If the organisation is a company, its articles of association may require directors to retire by rotation after a certain amount of time on the board (their 'term limit'), and the board needs to be mindful of this.

Succession planning should be addressed by the board as a whole, or delegated to a nomination committee where relevant, for approval by the board. In its recruitment policy, the board (or its nomination committee, if there is one) will need to consider any skills gaps which may arise after the retirement of a board member. The board can predict who is due for retirement by rotation, and plan for any resulting skills gaps accordingly.

Arts organisations often have board members who serve for many years; these may be founder members or directors who have not been required to retire by rotation at the end of their term. Good governance recommends that the board rotate its members within a defined timeframe. Furthermore, funders usually recommend that a board be refreshed and updated to allow new ideas and strategies to come forward.

Setting Strategy

The board of directors should play a major role in setting strategy,[19] as well as "formulating high-level objectives; allocating resources; and providing guidance, direction, and accountability for management".[20] The recommendation that the board set strategy applies particularly to arts organisations, which, though often small, have a large societal influence, and whose essence is to create as much art as possible with the budget available. This results in the arts organisation having to continuously stretch its resources, meaning that its board's oversight role is important, providing the skill and professional knowledge to review and direct strategy and its implementation. In setting strategy, the board is positioned, through its individual members, to bring artistic, financial, legal, management and

---

[19] See Deloitte Development LLC, "Hot Topics – Improving board effectiveness: Oversight of strategy" (2012).

[20] KPMG LLP *et al.*, "Enhancing Board Oversight: Avoiding Judgment Traps and Biases" (Committee of Sponsoring Organisations of the Treadway Commission, 2012).

other skills to bear. In reviewing progress against the agreed strategy at regular meetings, the board can then propose measures to bring the organisation into alignment.

Strategy and 'Short-termism'

A feature of funded arts organisations is that any strategy is usually dependent on receiving sufficient money to carry out the artistic programmes. Since funding is agreed annually, setting strategy beyond one year can be speculative, though necessary, as artistic programming often needs to be organised over a number of years. This leads to uncertainty in the organisation, for example when programme changes are needed, if funding is cut. One solution to this short-termism problem is to diversify sources of funding and reduce dependency on a single source.

An initiative by the Arts Council called RAISE aims to place arts organisations on a stronger financial footing by supporting them in raising private finance. This initiative found that income from private fundraising by arts organisations in Ireland is less than 3% of their total income.[21]

Effective Board Meetings

Funders will often stipulate a requirement for regular board meetings and ask to be copied in on the minutes as this gives them a view on how their money is being spent and any problems being encountered. Most of the guidelines for the arts sector (e.g. the Arts Council's "Practical Guide for Board Members of Arts Organisations") recommend monthly board meetings. In addition:

- The meetings should have an agenda issued in advance, with sufficient time for board members to read it thoroughly before the meeting.
- The chairman selected for the meetings should be a board member who is competent in chairing meetings in a timely and efficient manner.
- The company secretary should be in attendance to take minutes and to fulfil other company secretarial duties.

---

[21] The RAISE: Building Fundraising Capacity pilot initiative offers one-to-one support to arts organisations for the thorough planning and implementation of tailored fundraising programmes (www.artscouncil.ie, accessed September 2014).

- As well as reflecting a good quality of debate and an openness to discussing key issues, the minutes should document appropriate actions, with dates for planned completion.
- Reports of subcommittees should be presented and discussed.
- Management accounts and cash positions need to be presented to the board at each meeting, or on a regular basis, and discussed at the meeting.

Financial Control

Financial control is driven from the board, but is often the weakest aspect of arts organisations. In cases of weak financial control, the skill of an accountant on the board is recommended.

A review of the organisation's finances should be included on the agenda for every board meeting, including a review of the budget and the management accounts. Few arts organisations have cash reserves and a frequent stipulation of funders is that grants be spent within a specific timeframe (usually one year). Overspending will also be seen as a negative factor by potential funders or regular funders who provide annual funding.[22] The board needs to ensure that the financial reporting is complete, timely and accurate because funders need clarity on how grant monies are being spent. For an arts organisation, a board with the right skills can make a significant contribution to its orderly financial operation.

Some of the funders I interviewed were clear that when organisational problems came to their attention, the best way to resolve them was by working with the board. In many cases, organisational problems were a symptom of misalignment at board level. Some funders retain the right to attend board meetings as a voting director and where there are difficulties or budget overruns, the funder may adopt the role of 'additional board member' and carry out informal due diligence or make attempts to 'fix' the problem, using their vote if necessary.

Indeed, funders of arts organisations have frequently reserved the right to sit on the board in order to address any financial issues that may arise. One funder stated: "If governance works well, the board is dynamic and the

---

[22] The Arts Council and the city and county councils are examples of regular funders of arts organisations. The Arts Council has a category called 'Regularly Funded Organisations' for organisations that receive annual funding.

board make-up is good. Sometimes when there are problems the solution is to strengthen the board."

Where an arts organisation is in financial difficulty, the board needs to meet to investigate the issue and agree plans to resolve it. In circumstances of financial difficulty, the steps outlined in **Chapter 4**, in the section on "Directors' Liabilities and Responsibilities in Difficult Times", may be useful for the board.

Risk Management

For larger commercial companies, keeping a 'risk register' to identify and manage organisational risks is considered good practice – and the same applies to arts organisations. Managing risk is further complicated for arts organisations by the need to balance the goal of achieving artistic excellence with inevitable exposure to financial risk.

Accountants on the boards of arts organisations who were interviewed for this book point out that they have the difficult task of supporting artistic endeavours while also making sure that the organisation spends within its budgetary limits. There is an ongoing dynamic between funding so-called 'pure art' and selling more popular forms of art which may earn more revenue. This is an ongoing conundrum for the finance functions of arts organisations, with some organisations stating that they need to take a controlled risk at least once a year in order to support outstanding artistic endeavour. This type of artistic endeavour usually carries a risk of creating a loss.

Whereas in the for-profit sector risks are taken with great frequency with each new product or service development and launch, for arts organisations funded by public monies, these decisions are more difficult and more public. Yet almost all arts-sector interviewees pointed out to me that great art is produced by taking risks. In such circumstances, it is the board's role to support executive management in taking controlled risks (which can be a very difficult dynamic for smaller organisations). The role of the board in deciding when and how to take a risk, and how to manage that risk, can be pivotal for the success of the artistic endeavour. The financial skills of the board are needed, as are regular project updates and management accounts. (Risk management in arts organisations is further discussed in **Chapter 7**.)

Conflicts of Interest

Company law provides some clarity on how conflicts of interest can arise for directors. A common potential conflict of interest is identified in the Companies Acts as relating to contracts:

> "It shall be the duty of a director of a company who is in any way, whether directly or indirectly, interested in a contract or proposed contract with the company to declare the nature of his interest at a meeting of the directors of the company."[23]

Other examples of conflicts of interest are where a board member sells goods or services or give loans to the company, either directly or through another company on whose board he or she also sits, and/or where a board member can make a financial gain or benefit from the transaction.

Similar conflicts of interest situations can arise on the boards of arts organisations where directors are also directors or executives of other organisations. For example, this can occur where the grant of funding to one organisation is subject to agreement by the board of another, and an individual director is a member of both boards.

Policies with regard to board members' conflicts of interest and procedures for their resolution should be set out in a board members' induction handbook. This is preferable to allowing conflicts of interest to be discussed at the boardroom table as they arise or are noticed. As Robinson and Wasserman point out: "Sometimes board members create conflicts of interest simply because they don't understand where the boundaries are, not out of deliberate deceit and greed."[24]

There are situations where a director can be sued (e.g. for a conflict of interest or lawsuits by ex-employees, suppliers or members), so it is good practice for arts organisations to indemnify their board directors by purchasing directors and officers liability insurance. For example, if a director is involved in a board decision to grant a contract to a third party, a disappointed vendor may challenge the decision by citing conflict of interest, even though no conflict occurred or the conflict was dealt with adequately by the board.

---

[23] Companies Act 1963, section 194(1).
[24] Robinson, A. and Wasserman, N., *The Board Member's Easier Than You Think Guide to Nonprofit Finances* (Emerson & Church, 2012).

Organisations can protect their directors with directors and officers liability insurance, meaning that the main risk for the directors in such circumstances is to their reputations.'

Board Rotation and Term Limits for Directors

Arts organisations are usually set up by enthusiastic and passionate individuals who eventually incorporate as a company. These individuals then become founder board members. Thus, the board is made up of like-minded people, who are often also friends. In these situations, control of the board is held by the founders. As the organisation succeeds and grows, however, a static, unchanging board can cause the company to stagnate.

Many studies have found that the retirement of directors by rotation is the best way of keeping a vibrant and dynamic board, as new board members contribute new ideas and viewpoints. Neil Pope argues that:

> "Board rotation processes and a six-year limit on the time anyone sits on a particular Board yields better Board performance and promotes a healthier relationship for Chief Executive and Board."[25]

Rotation of the chairperson should follow the same rules and the board itself should be charged with enforcing the term limits.

The normal term of office for a director should be clearly explained in the board policy documents; the board members' induction handbook, board induction courses and documents should outline the term of office for which a newly elected board member is expected to serve. Such documents should also state the circumstances under which a director can be re-elected and should also specify clearly the limit to the number of terms for which any director can sit on the board. Two terms of three years is deemed too much in some commentaries. In my opinion, board members should expect to serve for one term only, and only in exceptional circumstances may they be re-elected to serve a second term.

---

[25] Pope, N., *A Boardroom Guide to Organisational Capacity Building: Overcoming the Management Deficit in Ireland's Not-For-Profit Sector* (2012). (http://www.2into3.com/_fileupload/A%20Boardroom%20Guide%20to%20Organisational%20Capacity%20Building%20Overcoming%20the%20Management%20Deficit%20in%20Irelands%20Not-for-Profit%20Sector.pdf., accessed June 2014.)

While it is relatively straightforward to set out policies for board appointments and member rotation, it can be difficult to implement them. For example, when an organisation is set up by founder members, all of whom sit on the board after the incorporation of the company, it can be difficult for the group, or for new members joining the group, to implement a board retirement policy with term limits. This is made much easier by having board policies and rules in place right from the outset and agreed by all members.

In *A Boardroom Guide to Organisational Capacity Building*, Neil Pope identifies four growth and development phases for organisations in the non-profit sector. Phase One involves setting up the organisation with a purpose and an operating board of directors. The organisation then grows to Phase Two, displaying entrepreneurial leadership and passionate association to its own cause; it has a homogenous board, often picked by the executive director.

When the organisation grows to Phase Three, it can be observed as having a diverse board, including professional experts and good working subcommittees, with formal processes for assessment of company and board performance, and a strong oversight of policy. Finally, Phase Four involves the mature, sustainable and innovative organisation, with the board focused on policy and composed of public and business leaders possessing international reputation and credibility.

Of course, arts organisations can become 'stuck' in any of these phases; those organisations need to change their board dynamics to advance and to grow. Pope identifies term limits for board members and their rigorous implementation as a way of becoming 'unstuck' from these growth phases. The orderly rotation and refreshing of the board through the contributions of new members is identified as vital for growth and maturity.

The Role of the Chairman

The main responsibilities of the chair of the board of an arts organisation can be adapted from the 'Higgs Report', *Review of the role and effectiveness of non-executive directors*. The chair of the board is responsible for:

- leadership of the board, ensuring its effectiveness in all aspects of its role and setting its agenda;
- ensuring the provision of accurate, timely and clear information to directors;

- ensuring effective communication with stakeholders;
- arranging the regular evaluation of the performance of the board, its committees and individual directors; and
- facilitating the effective contribution of non-executive directors and ensuring constructive relations between executive and non-executive directors.[26]

The Higgs Report states that "the chairman has the responsibility of leading the board in setting the values and standards of the company and of maintaining a relationship of trust with and between the executive and non-executive members."[27] Higgs emphasises that the role of chairman is different from that of ordinary board members. The chairman is uniquely positioned as a communications channel between the board and the chief executive, and the board and stakeholders. In arts organisations researched for this book, the role of the chairman is viewed by funders as setting standards and values for the organisation and ensuring the smooth running of the organisation.

The board also has the power to recruit the chief executive, who is in turn answerable to the board. Good governance requires separation of the roles of chairman and chief executive. Boards of small arts organisations that still have founder members with controlling influences can tend to have the same person holding these roles; often this is simply a convenient option. However, it limits the effectiveness of the board, not just by reducing the diversity and scale of varying influences but by concentrating too much control in one board member. I would urge such organisations to recruit a separate chairman of the board, particularly when fundraising and large grant applications are planned. A governance audit or due diligence is often required by funders prior to grant giving, and many arts organisations will need to show that they are well governed.

Board Papers

The chair of the board should set and maintain standards for board papers, including minutes, agendas, schedules, etc. Board papers should be sent to board members a number of days in advance of meetings (five to seven days

---

[26] Adapted from Higgs, D., *Review of the role and effectiveness of non-executive directors* (2003).

[27] *Ibid.*

in advance is reasonable). Those days should include a weekend to allow board members to have time to read the papers thoroughly.

Additional board papers should be sent only on an exceptional basis. It is difficult for board members, especially voluntary members, to schedule unexpected additional time before meetings to read unscheduled papers. The extra papers can also lead to disorganisation and confusion in the agenda.

Board papers should follow a standard format, including:

- Minutes of the last meeting, to be agreed by all board members present at the meeting and to be approved by the chair.
- An agenda with structured items for discussion, which should include discussion of the financial outcomes to date, any forecasts and a report of cash flow availability (if this is important).
- Schedules backing up any important agenda items for further explanation and detail, e.g. draft budget papers or financial analysis.
- A planned/suggested date for the next board meeting.

There has been debate as to whether agendas should include an item for 'any other business' (AOB). If AOB is scheduled as the last agenda item, there can be a tendency for the board to view AOB as signalling the end of the meeting, and thus the opportunity to raise any other issues is rushed and sometimes sacrificed in the interests of ending a long meeting. There are no perfect solutions to this problem, but the following is useful:

- the chairman can table AOB at the beginning of the meeting;
- the chairman can ask for items to be tabled for AOB just before the meeting; or
- AOB can be omitted on the basis that the chairman invites 'other business' issues to be discussed at some point during the meeting.

The key driver is the quality of communication and cohesiveness of the board, as each member needs to clearly understand their duties and rights to be heard at board meetings and to raise the issues they consider to be important.

Summary

Boards are dynamic, unique to the organisation and dependent on a good mix of trust and respect amongst its members. Good, basic rules for the board's operation help it to be the most effective in directing and governing the organisation. Beneath this layer are the values, culture and ethics of the organisation; these are also influenced, or perhaps even determined, by the board.

Much study and thought is currently being put into board dynamics and board influence. For example, where organisations are important to the society or community in which they operate, it is important to ask whether the board should be representative of that society or community. What is the best mix between necessary skills and representation? None of these questions is clear cut, and perhaps they are dependent on the particular organisation or circumstances.

For arts organisations, the problem is often finding good and conscientious board members. The procedures for the recruitment of new board members in **Appendix 1** may be of assistance. Given the trust, relationship-building and organisational issues involved, however, there is no one-size-fits-all approach to board recruitment.

Some board members who may appear indifferent can be excellent in crises; some who are clearly bored with routine are excellent in times of great change; some represent the community, and some are excellent accountants. As in life, we would like to have it all, but arts organisations would be very lucky to get it all. A dynamic, adaptive and frequently refreshed approach will, however, put the organisation on a good path to having an effective board.

Boards also need to be responsive to changing landscapes for funding, and need to be able to use their mix of skills and expertise to identify forces that could change their business models. The changing landscape for funding in Ireland is affecting the business models of our arts organisations. This represents a change in policy: those organisations are being encouraged to look for funding in different ways and from different sources, and this will have fundamental implications for the arts sector. These implications will be addressed in the next chapter.

Chapter 6

The Changing Business Models and Governance Programmes

We always overestimate the change that will occur in the next two years
and underestimate the change that will occur in the next ten. Don't let
yourself be lulled into inaction.

Bill Gates

Introduction

As arts organisations implement governance codes and better governance
standards, their business models and funding landscapes are also changing.
In Ireland, we have long cherished our 'arm's-length' principle of funding, in
contrast to the American model of private, individual contributions to the
arts driven by low government funding and tax breaks. However, the funding model in Ireland is shifting direction and in this chapter we will compare,
and endeavour to inform, this changing approach with arts funding models
developed elsewhere in the world, notably in the US.

We will also discuss what an appropriate programme for corporate governance might look like in this changing landscape for funding and managing
arts organisations, and we will examine the policy implications for arts
organisations depending more on fundraising and philanthropic donations.

Due to recent developments in government and Arts Council policies, the
typical Irish funding model for the arts is changing. The Arts Council's
strategic overview, *Developing the Arts in Ireland: 2011–2013*, declares that
it will "seek to maximise public and private investment in the arts through
maintaining and developing funding partnerships, through seeking new
sources and new means of support – public, corporate and philanthropic –
and through encouraging arts organisations to broaden their income
base".[1] The increased encouragement for arts organisations to fundraise
and to diversify their income streams is making it necessary for those
organisations to change their funding models.

---

[1] The Arts Council, *Developing the Arts in Ireland 2011–2013* (2011).

In the face of this development, the merits and demerits of funding models in other countries are being considered by Irish arts organisations and their funders. The value of the arts and the policy implications behind the funding models are discussed below.

As the business and organisational models for arts organisations change from being funded by a single governmental source to funding from a number of diverse sources, organisations will need to understand:

- what will be expected of them under new funding guidelines/new private funders;
- how to manage this new dynamic;
- the opportunities that the changed business models present; and
- how to assess the implications for their organisation and their artistic output.

Arts organisations will also need to be vigilant and outspoken about any impacts on artistic quality and freedom, as they are the guardians of one of our national treasures – our cultural heritage.

The new 'mixed model' for funding is predicted to perceptibly shift us from the 'arm's-length principle' (see below) and move us closer to the US model. This will produce different outcomes for our arts organisations, which will need to identify possible effects on artistic outcomes as a result of the funding changes. Will they curb artistic independence? Will the arm's-length principle of funding be compromised, and will this make our art more or less elitist or populist? This question is a much larger, societal one, which examines our cultural policies and core beliefs, and is discussed below.

The Irish Model for Funding the Arts

The traditional model for funding the arts in Ireland is based on the model established by John Maynard Keynes in 1942, when he took office as Chairman of the Council for the Encouragement of Music and the Arts (CEMA). (CEMA became Arts Council England in 1994.) The Arts Council of Ireland was established in 1951 and is based on the English model. It describes itself as "the national agency for funding, developing and promoting the arts in Ireland". It is "an autonomous body, which is under the aegis of the Department of Arts, Heritage & Gaeltacht".[2]

---

[2] www.artscouncil.ie.

The Arts Council is funded by the Irish Government, and in times of governmental cutbacks the Arts Council's funds are also being reduced (i.e. €63.2 million in 2012, down from €65.2 million in 2011).[3] These funds are given as grant-in-aid to the Arts Council and are then distributed by the Arts Council. This practice of distancing government from an institution that it created and finances came to be known as the **'arm's-length principle'** in the 1970s,[4] and was originally established by Keynes as a fair and non-judgemental way of funding the arts.

The Arm's-length Principle

In 1924, John Maynard Keynes, then Bursar of King's College, Cambridge, had observed the University Grants Committee voting for "distribution without strings"[5] to each university. Keynes reinterpreted this as arm's-length grant funding. This was the model Keynes used in 1941 as a framework in the Council for the Encouragement of Music and the Arts (CEMA). This arm's-length system safeguarded the arts from undue political influence or propaganda, as had happened in Nazi Germany. In a speech given in Dublin in 1933, Keynes issued a warning on the dangers of economic nationalism: "The worst risk of all ... is intolerance and the stifling of instructed criticism."[6] His philosophy of liberal debate and balancing forces in what he called "the new economic modes" permeated his views: "Now for this process bold, free and remorseless criticism is a *sine qua non* of ultimate success."[7]

Additionally, the system was at arm's length from accountability by politicians. More than 50 years later, Dame Liz Forgan, former Chair of Arts Council England, stated of the arm's-length principle that: "It protects politicians from being held accountable for the occasionally outrageous, offensive or otherwise troublesome work of artists."[8] It also protects artists from being unduly influenced or controlled by their funders.

---

[3] The Arts Council Annual Report and Accounts, 2011 and 2012.
[4] Upchurch, A.R. (quoting Hewson, 1995), "John Maynard Keynes, the Bloomsbury Group and the Origins of the Arts Council Movement" (2004) Vol. 10, No. 2, *International Journal of Cultural Policy*, 203–17.
[5] *Ibid.*
[6] Keynes, J.M., "National Self-Sufficiency" (1933) Vol. 22, No. 4, *The Yale Review*, 755–69.
[7] *Ibid.* Keynes was referring to the process of bringing the "new economic modes" into being.
[8] Dame Liz Forgan, TMA Winder Event speech (www.uktheatre.org, accessed September 2014).

Part of the system Keynes instituted for funding the arts was the practice of peer review, which he believed was fair and equitable, and in which no one artist or art type was favoured. The peer review system involves a panel of artists evaluating the work of other artists for grant applications. In Keynes's framework, this was a way of keeping professional standards as high as possible. This peer review system is now used by the Arts Council of Ireland. Quoted in *The Irish Times*, Patrick Murphy, Director of the Royal Hibernian Academy, points out that: "The members of the Arts Council are artistic peers made up of scholars, artists, writers, dramatists and audience. So to receive a grant is to receive the judgement of your peers. That's the core, beyond the financial investment of a bursary or a grant, that judgement has value."[9]

The Irish system of funding the arts is effectively the same system as the one designed by Keynes. The system is not directly accountable to central government, making it one of the most independent arts funding systems in the world. It provides relative artistic freedom for artists by keeping their funding at arm's length from direct government influence. Grants for the arts are given by a "semi-autonomous and non-governmental body"[10] relatively free from political interference; in Ireland, that body is the Arts Council.

'Regularly Funded Organisations'

The arm's-length system can also lead to dependency on funding with the creation of so-called 'regularly funded organisations'. Keynes envisaged that arm's-length grants to arts organisations would not be sustained indefinitely: "Keynes saw grants and subsidies as a temporary measure, the need for which over time would wither away."[11] This viewpoint came from a business objective of nurturing ventures until they were mature and self-sustainable. However, arts organisations that define themselves as non-profit necessarily spend all of their income and are not seeking financial independence from their funders. They therefore need regular funding.

---

[9] Tipton, G., "The artists who stay out in the cold", *The Irish Times*, 1 February 2013.

[10] Upchurch, A.R., "Keynes's Legacy: An Intellectual's Influence Reflected in Arts Policy" (2011) Vol. 17, No. 1, *International Journal of Cultural Policy*, 69–80.

[11] Peacock, A., *Paying the Piper: Culture music and money* (Edinburgh University Press, 1993) as cited by Upchurch, A.R., "John Maynard Keynes, the Bloomsbury Group and the Origins of the Arts Council Movement" (2004) Vol. 10, No. 2, *International Journal of Cultural Policy*, 203–17.

Although regular funding for arts organisations was not encouraged by Keynes, it is a reality for many large Irish arts organisations that, because they are regularly funded, fundraise from the private sector only as a secondary source of funding. Although they suffer from Arts Council cutbacks in recessionary times, they do remain independent and avoid being unduly influenced or controlled by private funders.

The Mixed System of Funding

Under threat of government funding cuts, the advantages of having a mixed system of funding are being revisited by government and the Arts Councils in both Ireland and England. In Ireland, funding from donations and endowments and non-government sources are being examined and encouraged by the Arts Council; this encouragement of seeking a variety of funding sources is seen as beneficial and promoting sustainability.

In support of the move towards a mixed system of funding for arts organisations, Alan Davey, Chief Executive of Arts Council England, has described the English system as "the mixed economy of funding from public and private sources":[12]

> "[W]e have the conditions for excellence in the arts in this country that are quite simply working. ... Key to these conditions are two things: the mixed economy of funding from public and private sources, where public investment is made to work hard; and the arm's length arrangements for providing central government funding for artists through an independent expert Arts Council."

With reduced government funding to the Arts Council, Davey makes the case for trying to "deliver more from the private sector, by improving fundraising skills and the overall culture of giving to the arts".

This mixed system of funding allows the flexibility to seek additional funding from private sources. A diversity of income sources is important in times of reduced government funding. As Arts Council England states in its 2010 report, *Endowment in the arts*: "Clearly no system is perfect, but the strength of the English mixed economy is that it shelters arts organisations, at least partially, from financial crises in any one strand of funding".[13]

---

[12] Alan Davey, Chief Executive, in *Achieving Great Art for Everyone: A Strategic Framework for Arts* (Arts Council England, 2010), p. 7.

[13] Arts Council England, *Endowment in the arts* (2010).

Thus, from a funding perspective, a mixed system of funding provides the arts with some insulation against reductions in funding from any one source; that is, provided that arts organisations are able to fundraise. In Ireland, this has not been the case; arts organisations have been slow to fundraise. Recognising this, the Arts Council has set up initiatives like the RAISE programme, which is designed to assist and enable arts organisations to raise funds.[14] The Arts Council announced that Irish arts organisations are generating more money from private investment. Noting the success of the RAISE programme, private investment increased from €2 million in 2012 to €2.5 million in 2013.[15]

Excellence or Elitism?

The very strength of the arm's length arts council is often perceived as its principle weakness. Fostering artistic excellence is often seen as promoting elitism, with respect to both type of art work produced and audience served.[16]

Instituting and supporting a system of arm's-length grant-giving governed by an arts council, with peer review by artists and artistic excellence as a goal, also and continuously raises the question of access for the public. Public criticism of how the Arts Council of Ireland allocates money to the arts highlights unresolved conflicts between artistic excellence and access.

In *The Case for Elitism,* Emer O'Kelly argues: "The god of 'access for all' has become a satanic destroyer of the imaginative leap." She suggests that if we only fund and promote art that is designed to be popular and accessible by all, we are in danger of losing the excellence, which is a feature of independent, challenging or avant-garde art, and continues:

> "It is the duty of the Arts Council to demand that the mix is tilted in favour of the great or potentially great art when it spends taxpayers' money. That means a close re-assessment of projects that more properly belong under

---

[14] In 2012, the Arts Council launched the RAISE: Building Fundraising Capacity pilot initiative. Professional one-to-one support is provided to selected organisations for two years through planning and implementing a tailored fundraising programme.

[15] "Art's Council's RAISE pilot reports increase in private funding" (2014) (www.artscouncil.ie, accessed September 2014).

[16] Hillman-Chartrand, H. and McCaughey, C., "The Arm's Length Principle and the Arts: An International Perspective – Past, Present and Future" in M.C. Cummings Jr and J. Mark Davidson Schuster (eds.), *Who's to Pay for the Arts: The International Search for Models of Support* (American Council for the Arts, 1989).

the banner of the Department of Community and Family affairs than under the banner of the Department of Arts, and a tilting in favour of the people who lead the way with great, or potentially great art."[17]

Excellent art is often 'before its time', and has limited popular, contemporary appeal. However, if most people don't like it, should it be funded by public monies? While this book will not attempt to examine the implied philosophical and social issues, it does ask the question: should we expect excellence in art or should art be popular and mirror current interests and beliefs?

Those who demand that art should be accessible by all argue that obscure, unpopular art is only for an artistic and intellectual elite; but those who demand excellence argue that art designed only to be popular and to echo received beliefs stifles creativity and innovation. Thus, the question is postulated over and over: is it art?

To date, the Arts Council has been by far the largest funder of the arts in Ireland. As we change to a more mixed system of funding, consideration needs to be given to the issues raised above. Furthermore, and importantly, does funding that is not at arm's-length compromise artistic integrity and excellence?

Direct fundraising can come with specific limitations, as criteria for obtaining funds have the potential to affect the artistic form. For example, direct funding from government can cut off funding to artists who criticise the funder. On the other hand, independent, individual funders have their own preferences – they may want to fund only certain art forms, e.g. opera or ballet. These are the considerations that our arts organisations now need to address in the framework of their missions and strategies. Examples of limitations being created by the funders are discussed further below.

Limiting the Range of Art Forms

Although in Ireland and England there is general agreement that the arts councils are a desirable and independent way of funding the arts, this funding method has been shown to limit the range of art forms by funding some art forms but not others. While the strength of the arm's-length system is its freedom from direct government intervention, this independence also seems

---

[17] O'Kelly, E., *The Case for Elitism* (The Arts Council, 2007).

to have contributed to a tendency to maintain the status quo. If only certain, established categories of art are funded, what will happen to new forms of art (e.g. graffiti) as they emerge (as jazz and photography did in the early 20th century) but are not recognised and supported?

A 2011 study by the Council of Europe found that, "Although the number of supported arts organisations grew, the range of forms supported was still narrow after 20 years (poetry, photography and jazz, for example, were not supported for many years)."[18] The arts councils have been accused of having a "relatively closed field of operation"[19]: "the emphasis on professional standards and excellence ... [has] allowed power to be held and exercised by an oligarchy operating in the Arts Council, and its regional offices."[20] This weakness in the system can limit access and limit the range of art forms eligible for funding.

Other Funding Models

The American funding model for funding the arts encourages and largely relies upon tax-efficient private donations, with a much smaller arts council, called the National Endowment for the Arts. The comparison with the Irish funding model is stark. In the US for 2013, the funding request to Congress for the National Endowment for the Arts was a mere $154 million in direct government funding, a tiny amount when compared to the arts councils in Europe.[21]

In 1989, cultural policy researchers Harry Hillman-Chartrand and Claire McCaughey analysed and described the funding models.[22] The arts funding models they identified are: the facilitator state, the patron state, the architect state and the engineer state. These models are useful indicators for the level of government involvement in culture and how cultural outputs are affected by government policy. These are succinctly summarised

---

[18] Council of Europe 2011, Chapter 1.

[19] Upchurch, A.R., "Keynes's Legacy: An Intellectual's Influence Reflected in Arts Policy" (2011) Vol. 17, No. 1, *International Journal of Cultural Policy*, 69–80.

[20] *Ibid.*

[21] "Today, the President released the details of his FY2013 budget request to Congress. This includes a $154.255 million request for the National Endowment for the Arts (NEA)" 13 February 2012 (http://www.nea.gov/news/news12/Budget.html, accessed 2 February 2013).

[22] Hillman-Chartrand, H. and McCaughey, C., "The Arm's Length Principle and the Arts: An International Perspective – Past, Present and Future".

by Michael A. Keane and Weihong Zhang in their article, "Cultural Creative Industries or Creative (Cultural) Industries?", as follows:

> **"The facilitator state** is the ideal 'hands-off' model: it entails indirect promotion of cultural activity through the extension of tax incentives and inducements to corporate institutions and philanthropic donors. In other words, the government provides the conditions that favour cultural production and consumption ...
>
> **[T]he patron state** ... In countries such as the United Kingdom, Canada and Australia [and Ireland] this tradition still prevails allowing the cultural sphere, usually the upper end of the arts, to be supported 'through arm's-length councils' which are usually 'quasi-independent bodies'. Decisions regarding financial support are subsequently based on criteria of 'excellence' determined by peer groups.
>
> **The architect model** allows government a more direct role in shaping the environment. It is thus more interventionist and is connected to social welfare and national cultural policy objectives. Critics of this approach contend that artists will seek to produce work that conforms to whatever the state favours at a particular time rather than asserting true creative independence. The best example of this approach is France.
>
> **The engineer model** is where government directly intervenes and controls the cultural sphere. Culture is an instrument of political education and the government owns the means of production including the media. The examples here are the former Soviet Union and China prior to the 1990s."[23]

Thus, the way in which the arts are funded greatly influences artistic output and capability.

The models first postulated by Hillman-Chartrand and McCaughey were further refined by Keane and Zhang, who made further distinctions and postulated four different models[24]:

---

[23] Keane, M. and Zhang, W., "Cultural creative industries or creative (cultural) industries?" in Hu, Huilin (eds.), *China's Cultural Industries Forum* (Shanghai People's Publishing, 2008). (Emphases added.)

[24] *Ibid.*

- The **welfare model**, in which the cultural industries have a "net negative economic impact on the economy", but the overall effect is regarded as "welfare positive".
- The **normal model** argues that "creative industries are not special" and for policy purposes they should be treated like any other industry.
- In the **growth model**, the creative industries are deemed to be a driver of growth, and creative industries are considered special because they "facilitate the growth of other sectors".
- The **creative economy** model holds that creative industries are elements of the innovation system of the whole economy.

In effect, rather than seeing cultural creative industries as an end in themselves, Keane and Zhang argue that creative cultural industries are the key to innovation, change, the "coordination of new ideas or technologies" and economic development. "These creative cultural industries will continue to play a key role in re-converting static forms of culture into interactive forms, they will drive economic growth, and they will promote diversity."[25]

Analysis of the various funding models allows us to predict possible outcomes for Ireland as we move towards the mixed funding approach, as discussed above. Awareness of these models helps to identify and decode the governmental policies underpinning arts funding. It also helps us to anticipate what the economy and society is expecting of the cultural industries, and it helps the cultural industries to identify what they can contribute.

Using such theories, we can identify the government funding model used in Ireland and identify the expected outcomes of that funding methodology. Ireland now seems closest to the creative economy model. In its 2010 report, *The Global Irish Economic Forum: One Year On*, the Irish Department of Foreign Affairs, writing about the Farmleigh Forum held in 2009, which marked a policy shift in relation to Ireland's cultural industries, uses concepts and language resonant of a creative economy model of arts funding:

> "The Farmleigh Forum demonstrated that for many people around the world, Irish and non-Irish alike, Ireland's rich cultural identity remains the defining characteristic of the Irish. It is this cultural association that Farmleigh helped to highlight and which the Government is determined to build upon …

[25] *Ibid.*

The arts and cultural community have welcomed and engaged very actively in this discussion, with a view to developing a strategy that can build on this new strategic priority and unlock the full potential of the critical and complex connection between culture, Ireland's international reputation, and business."[26]

Here, culture is connected to national reputation and business interests, a connection which overlays the previous identification, that of culture enhancing society and the democratic process (as per the Keynesian model), and/or producing "great, or potentially great art", as argued by Emer O'Kelly. Irish society has shifted in terms of how we view the arts, how we engage with our cultural industries and what we expect from artistic and cultural outputs. This is of great significance for the debate around governance and its importance in the arts sector. If funding the arts is now being seen as a lever for our economic success, fundraising for the arts becomes necessary as an enabler for more artistic output, which will lead to more innovation, change and advancement. If these arguments are materialised, arts organisations can expect to receive reasonable funding in times of severe funding shortage. However, arts organisations must be accountable and be able to demonstrate how those funds are being used to support their visions and, by extension, their benefits as drivers of innovation and change – and this will be both good and bad for the sector.

Summary

We tend to justify our expenditure on the arts by quoting numbers based on people employed in the sector, inward cultural tourism or the monetary value of the sector.[27] However, in looking for financial quantification, we risk losing sight of our core belief that art creates meaning in modern society, or to quote from Elliot Eisner: "A culture populated by a people whose imagination is impoverished, has a static future. In such a culture there will be little change because there will be little sense of possibility."[28]

Implicit in the governance discussion is the question of the materiality of the arts sector and how important it is to our economy and its influence on

---

[26] Department of Foreign Affairs, *The Global Irish Economic Forum: One Year On. A report on the follow up to the Global Irish Economic Forum at Farmleigh* (2010).

[27] Such as in "Assessment of the Economic Impact of the Arts in Ireland" (Indecon International Economic Consultants for the Arts Council of Ireland, November 2011).

[28] Eisner, E., *The Arts and the Creation of Mind* (Yale University Press, 2002).

our society. The arts are instrumental in adding value through cultural tourism, building inclusiveness by having public participation in audiences and visits to cultural venues. It has also been shown to have enormous therapeutic value to sick or distressed people; and art has long been used in crime prevention and in learning.

However, there is also an intrinsic value in producing art for its own sake which must not be forgotten. It is the production of ground-breaking art that in many ways defines a culture and makes a society worth remembering. We define many of the societies of the past by the artefacts they have left. Similarly, we also judge societies by a dearth of enduring artefacts or by their censorship of the arts.

For these reasons, any evaluations of arts organisations must be qualified. A for-profit organisation can show its worth by its share price and its profits, but arts organisations cannot be so easily judged, because their measurement necessarily includes assessment of their values.

Our governmental policies towards the arts have shifted: funding for the arts now comes with an expectation of increased innovation, increased change and increased cooperation. The policy shift that underpins these funding changes also demands increased corporate governance (with visibility, accountability and transparency). It is important that we remain critical of our policy towards arts funding to ensure that our society does not lose sight of how important art is in the way we define *who we are.*

Chapter 7

Managing Risk in Arts Organisations

Is it feasible, or even desirable, for nonprofit organisations to be accountable to everyone for everything?

Alnoor Ebrahim[1]

Introduction

While all organisations, large and small, need to comply with the basic principles of good corporate governance, the governance framework should also be adapted for the needs of smaller organisations. Arts organisations cannot afford to ignore corporate governance practices just because they are small; and it is becoming increasingly common for the media to focus attention on governance failures in relatively small arts organisations. This is partly because so many arts organisations receive and spend public monies, and partly because they are visible and influential, despite their size and budgets.

This chapter discusses the implementation of additional governance best practices as applied to larger organisations, namely the identification and management of risk, and how those practices can be refined for smaller organisations. Some options for risk management are presented, and they are discussed within the 'comply or explain' framework, which, as we saw in **Chapter 3**, requires that organisations identify the governance code with which they want to comply and where they do not comply, explain why. Explaining non-compliance in this way improves transparency. In a governance statement in the annual report, addressing these issues helps to build trust with stakeholders. It also shows a healthy regard for best practice and a robust desire for good corporate governance.

Of course, embracing the spirit of good corporate governance involves more than simply declaring non-compliance in the annual report. Arts organisations wishing to address governance and to show that they are well governed should endeavour to understand and apply the *principles* behind the governance codes and the legislation. There is a general consensus that

[1] Ebrahim, A., "The Many Faces of Nonprofit Accountability (Working Paper No. 10-069)" (Harvard Business School, 2010).

good governance comes from the board, and in her research Johanne Turbide has shown that "bad governance can precipitate [financial] crises".[2] This will be discussed in the overall context of board effectiveness in identifying and dealing with risk in arts organisations.

Risk and the Arts

The arts organisations I interviewed were clear that taking risks is an important part of being innovative and successful. Indeed, risk is inherent in the operation of arts organisations. For example, there is the risk that audiences may not appear in sufficient numbers to performances. This can often be dependent on a bad review, or on other events running at the same time, or simply the weather. For the visual arts there is the risk that the public or major funders will not like what they see – the headline of an article in the *Irish Independent* of 31 October 2012 is self-explanatory: "Artist who refused to be gagged withdraws from council exhibit".

There is a whole range of other risks that can face arts organisations, such as health and safety, tax compliance and legal risks in relation to copyright and other forms of intellectual property (for example, there is an EC Directive on the resale rights for the benefit of the author of an original work of art).[3]

Reputation is perhaps the biggest asset of an art organisation, and reputational risks need to be identified and managed appropriately. The implementation of corporate governance programmes can reduce reputational risks by demanding good internal controls, managing financial risks and safeguarding stakeholders' funds.

Definition of Risk

A good definition of risk can be paraphrased from the definition used by Dublin City Council in its Financial Regulations: "A possible loss or other adverse consequence that has the potential to impact on an organisation's ability to achieve its objectives and fulfil its mission."[4] Dublin City Council has an active and vibrant arts programme and it is a significant funder of the

---

[2] Turbide, J., "Can Good Governance Prevent Financial Crises in Arts Organizations?" (2012) Vol. 14, No. 2, *International Journal of Arts Management*, 4–16.

[3] EC Directive 2001/84/EC.

[4] Dublin City Council Financial Regulations, 2007.

sector (see the survey of grant givers in **Appendix 8**); its identification of risk management might apply to arts organisations throughout the sector.

The same document also suggests a process for managing risk. This four-stage process is basic and should be easy to implement in arts organisations. The adage "what gets measured gets done" should be kept in mind. It is recommended that arts organisations identify, assess, manage and review their risks.

- **Identification of risk:** key risks that may prevent the achievement of the objectives set out in the corporate and business plans should be identified.
- **Assessment of risk:** risks should be assessed to determine their overall likelihood and potential impact on the organisation.
- **Management of risk:** there are a number of approaches to the management of risk, including tolerating the risk, treating the risk (i.e. controls), transferring the risk to a third party (i.e. insurance) or terminating it.
- **Review and reporting:** risk management is a continuously evolving and changing process and requires ongoing monitoring, reviewing, reporting and updating.[5]

We will examine how to build this risk management process into an organisation, and how the board can direct the process. There are big advantages to identifying and managing risk – in arts organisations, the very process of identifying risks can make the organisation aware of its risk appetite, and the different forms of risk it seeks to minimise.

Risk Strategy and Management

Arts organisations take risks, which sometimes can lose them money. The identification of an organisation's risk strategy – and risk appetite – will allow these risks to be clearly managed and to take place in a relatively more 'controlled' environment. If losses occur, a clear risk management plan will ensure that the losses do not jeopardise the overall financial health or viability of the organisation, and that there are mitigating events that will re-stabilise it. For example, where a show is a 'flop' or an exhibition gets negative media coverage, the risk management strategy will identify 'safer' revenue-generating programmes for the remainder of the year or until the organisation has returned to financial stability.

---

[5] *Ibid.*

An effective risk management process will identify and assess risk prior to the agreement of the artistic programme. Though comprehensive risk management documents for Irish arts organisations are hard to find, some guidelines from the *Code of Practice for the Governance of State Bodies* are suggested below. These echo the stages in the standard risk management cycle outlined above and provide some operational guidelines, as follows:

- Make risk management a standing management meeting agenda item.
- Consider establishing a risk committee, or including it in the charter of the audit committee (audit committees are discussed later in this chapter).
- Seek out risk management experience and expertise in the competencies of at least one board director. Arts organisations generally identify the artistic director as most appropriate for this role, as the artistic programming carries the highest inherent risk.
- For operational risks, including the artistic programme, appoint a chief risk officer or empower someone from the management team, and provide for a direct reporting line to the board. Health and safety and legal compliance can also be this person's responsibility.
- Approve the risk management policy, set the organisation's risk appetite, and approve the risk management business plan (including risk register) at least once a year.
- Review management reporting on risk management and note/approve actions as appropriate.
- Require periodic external review of the effectiveness of the risk management framework.[6]

An example of a strategic risk in an arts organisation would be where some of the directors of a theatre company decide to pursue an amateur agenda alongside the organisation's professional one. Amateur performances attract a different audience, so advertising requirements will have to be adjusted based on the target audience. This creates a difficulty for the board in having a cohesive vision and purpose, as well as in defining the mix of programmes. Funding thus becomes complicated as some funders (e.g. the Arts Council) do not fund amateurs. If the strategic risks of engaging in amateur productions have been identified before the programme starts, it will be easier for the board to track the programme's progress and respond to issues as they arise.

---

[6] Department of Finance, *Code of Practice for the Governance of State Bodies* (2009).

Operational Risks Particular to Arts Organisations

Some risks are specific to arts organisations, and some risks are common to all organisations but are particularly worrisome for arts organisations. Breach of intellectual property rights and non-compliance with the health and safety code are risks about which arts organisations and representative groups express particular concern. They are concerned not just with the operational risks involved but also with the risk of not achieving full compliance with the legislation governing these risks. The need for such compliance is an ongoing concern for arts organisations. The identification, management and review of these risks will help mitigate the dangers of non-compliance and the potential for financial and/or reputational damage as well as injury.

Copyright Infringement

Breach of intellectual property rights is a particularly sensitive risk for the arts sector and there are many examples of artists defending their artistic copyright. For example, a case arose in January 2013 regarding the Abbey Theatre. The case concerned a reworked version of Synge's classic play, *The Playboy of the Western World*. To mark the 100th anniversary of the play, Bisi Adigun and Roddy Doyle co-wrote an updated version of the iconic play. After an initial run in 2007, the Abbey Theatre ran the production again in 2008 and 2009. Adigun claimed that there were 120 changes to the script co-written by him in the version staged in 2008 and 2009. According to reports in the *Irish Examiner* (30 January 2013), he had sued the Abbey Theatre for copyright infringement, alleging a "distorted version" of the play had been restaged.

There are some organisations that help to protect and promote intellectual property rights in Ireland. For example, the Irish Visual Artists Rights Organisation (IVARO) provides for "the protection and promotion of the copyright of visual artists and their heirs".[7] IVARO manages the rights of its members through copyright licensing and artists' resale right services. It also implements the regulations of the European Communities (Artist's Resale Right) Regulations 2006, and Irish copyright laws.

Copyright is an emotive subject for artists, which can be gauged from an article published by Visual Artists Ireland on its website:

---

[7] www.ivaro.ie (accessed 10 May 2014).

"Copyright is about democracy. A democracy is an open society in which many voices can be heard, many visions can flourish. For such a society to sustain and renew itself, it must take great care of its creative, intellectual and artistic ecosystem. If this ecosystem is inhabited only by big corporate beasts, it will quickly become a wasteland. By protecting the multiplicity and diversity of creative actors, copyright helps to fertilise the ground from which an open society – one which continually challenges itself with new images and ideas – renews itself."[8]

An ongoing risk of working with artists is that of infringing their intellectual property rights. Arts organisations need to be particularly careful in addressing this risk and in avoiding breaches of the legislation. The reputational risks are high and it further damages an organisation's reputation to be sued by an artist. The financial risk of losing such a lawsuit can also be considerable and highly disruptive when, for example, organisations are required to withdraw artistic images or disallowed the use of published materials.

Health and Safety Breach

A further area of high risk for arts organisations is compliance with the health and safety code. Under the Safety, Health and Welfare at Work Act 1989, all employers are required to prepare a safety statement. The Arts Council provides guidance for arts organisations' health and safety issues in *The Arts and Health Handbook: A Practical Guide*. Full compliance with the legislation should be included in the consideration of risk and made part of the organisation's risk management strategy. Breaches of the health and safety code can cause injury to employees and the public, and therefore carry a significant reputational and financial risk. Organisations are advised to take out public and employee liability insurance to insure against the risk of being sued for accidents.

Risk Management and Audit Committees

How is risk identified and dealt with at board level? And how does a board discharge its duties in relation to risk management? These governance

---

[8] From www.irishequity.ie, accessed in September 2014, quoting Fintan O'Toole in *The Irish Times*.

questions relate partly to the finance and audit subcommittee of the board. Often it is this subcommittee that is charged by the board with including the risk portfolio in its terms of reference. This is partly because risk reporting often forms part of the directors' report in the financial statements and because risk management tends to work closely with the finance function.

Arts organisations often do not have an audit committee, as they tend to be too small in size and/or the finance committee takes the brief of an audit committee. The Companies Bill 2012 requires that large companies establish an audit committee. ('Large' is defined as having a balance sheet total exceeding €25 million, or a turnover exceeding €50 million, thereby excluding most of Ireland's arts organisations from the statutory requirement to establish an audit committee.)

Nevertheless, the statutory requirement is an indicator of best practice and many governance codes recommend having an audit committee. Audit committees are useful for monitoring controls and for planning the audit with the auditors, including receiving the management letter and holding an end-of-audit meeting. This board liaison with auditors at the pre-audit stage allows the board to voice any concerns to the auditors, which the auditors can then take into consideration when planning their work. At the post-audit meetings, the audit committee can represent the board in receiving the management letter and holding final discussions with the auditors.

For all but the smallest of organisations, the role of the finance committee can become onerous if it includes finance, risk and audit in its terms of reference. The audit committee, outlined below, includes the risk management oversight in its brief. Usually, in small arts organisations, finance and audit are merged into a single committee with some brief from the board on the oversight of risk management.

Where an organisation has an audit committee, it is useful and transparent to include a comment in the annual report that the committee exists and to discuss its terms of reference. This can include a paragraph on the audit committee and its membership, how often it convenes and a brief summary of its terms of reference and how it is constituted. The audit committee needs to be seen to be independent, its members independently selected and suitably qualified. It should review corporate governance statements in the annual report relating to the audit and to risk management.

The responsibilities of the audit committee are listed in the Companies Bill 2012, and in the Financial Reporting Council's *Guidance on Audit Committees* (2012), and are adapted below for arts organisations:

Without prejudice to the responsibility of the board of directors, the responsibilities of the audit committee shall include:

(a) the monitoring of the financial reporting process;
(b) the monitoring of the effectiveness of the company's systems of internal control and risk management;
(c) the monitoring of the statutory audit of the company's statutory financial statements; and
(d) reporting to the board on how it has discharged its responsibilities.

In relation to (d) above, the audit committee should report to the board on how it has discharged its responsibilities, including:

• the significant issues that it considered in relation to the financial statements and how those issues were addressed;
• its assessment of the effectiveness of the external audit process and its recommendation on the appointment or reappointment of the external auditor (not forgetting that it is good practice to rotate the auditors every three years); and
• any other issues on which the board has requested the committee's opinion.[9]

The monitoring and reporting of risk strategy and risk management by the audit committee is part of effective oversight of risk by the board. For arts organisations, whether or not risk and audit are part of the remit of the finance committee or whether risk management should stay on the agenda for both management and board meetings are important considerations.

Summary

Previous chapters set out working definitions of corporate governance and the implementation of governance structures in arts organisations. This chapter has argued that risk management and its ownership by the board is an important part of the corporate governance agenda. While arts organisations can adapt risk management frameworks from the business sector and from universally accepted risk management practices, there are certain risks that are of greater importance to arts organisations and may need to be separately noted and managed.

[9] Adapted from FRC, *Guidance on Audit Committees* (September 2012).

For arts organisations that are publicly funded, the identification and management of risk enables them to demonstrate their careful and prudent stewardship of public monies. In circumstances where risks do materialise and things go wrong, those organisations will remain fundable by showing good and effective risk management policies and by having risk-mitigating procedures in place to protect the assets of the company, including its good reputation.

Inherent risks in arts organisations arise not only from the operation of the organisation, but also from specific issues like copyright infringement and break of the health and safety code. The corporate governance initiatives discussed here can be used to further expand governance programmes, or to identify governance areas requiring further attention.

Arts organisations are protective of artistic integrity and the balance between better regulation, governance, the nurturing of talent and artistic expression. These reasonable concerns can be addressed with a well-balanced corporate governance programme that is aligned with organisational strategy and objectives. The programme can be rendered and reduced to fit the size of the organisation and to enable the governance programme to be embedded in its daily operations.

Because boards of directors are responsible for the governance of their organisations, they are also responsible for ensuring that the organisation has robust and effective risk management strategies in place. However, organisations interviewed were clear that successful arts organisations take risks in the production of great art, new artistic works or controversial work. For our arts and cultural organisations, the inherent risk of artistic failure is fundamental. It is partially through this risk that we identify the success of our arts organisations; indeed, if arts organisations take no risks, then the artistic output can be bland. The failure of a theatre production, or the controversy arising from visual art, are aspects of the creative crucible that define the excitement and interest we value in our arts organisations. It is vital, therefore, to identify these risks and work with them, to enable those risks to be defining, rather than destructive.

Chapter 8

Corporate Governance and Fundraising

*More and more business leaders recognize that their traditional
management recipes are providing insufficient guidance on how to
handle changing societal expectations around the globe.*
**International Finance Corporation,
World Bank Group (2009)**

Introduction

As we have seen, the funding models for arts organisations are changing, as are
the economic policies underpinning these models. Many organisations are in
fact well governed, but they do not make this visible to stakeholders in response
to these significant changes. There have been very few big financial scandals in
Irish arts organisations, but shifts in funding policy suggest that arts organisations now need to account for, prove and demonstrate good governance. They
can no longer expect funders to assume that governance is adequate simply
because no scandals from the arts sector have entered the public domain.

Fundraising in Ireland is relatively underdeveloped and under-researched.
Arts organisations are therefore entering an arena in which experience and
know-how is sparse. Yet in the changing economic climate, as effective fundraising becomes more necessary, the link between good governance and
fundraising becomes more important. This chapter discusses corporate governance in the context of fundraising.

Fundraising in Ireland: A Brief Literature Review

In 2002, the Ireland Funds produced a report called *Fostering Fundraising
in Ireland*, which noted the shortage of data on fundraising in Ireland[1]

---

[1] The Ireland Funds, *Fostering Fundraising in Ireland* (2002): "Data in relation to fundraising
in the Republic of Ireland are drawn from a series of research reports conducted by the
Policy Research Centre, National College of Ireland, and relates mainly to the period
1997/98. No current research data are available for the Republic."

and called for a "resource or entity which would provide a platform for the strategic development of the sector."[2] In the meantime, the Centre for Nonprofit Management at Trinity College Dublin had been founded in 2001 with an establishment grant from Atlantic Philanthropies. The Centre Nonprofit Management published a report in 2007 on the practice and scale of charitable fundraising in Ireland,[3] which highlighted the importance of fundraising in Irish charitable organisations and quantified the importance of the sector: "An analysis of 960 respondent fundraising organisations showed that they raised €193 million in 2004."[4] The same report quantified the importance of fundraising to the income of charitable organisations: "It has been estimated that charities rely on fundraising for 11% of overall income."[5] This study is of particular importance in the current economic climate, where arts organisations are being encouraged and enabled to fundraise in order to augment direct grant income.

A further study by Siobhán McGee and Freda Donoghue, entitled "The Conundrum of Fundraising in Nonprofit Organisations",[6] points out that: "[c]haritable status does not yet exist in Ireland".[7] ('Charitable status' is only recognised in tax law where certain organisations are given 'CHY' tax status and certain tax incentives.) McGee and Donoghue also identify "considerable informality in the sector",[8] and argue that the sector is underdeveloped and has "the need to develop fundraising practice".[9] This means that Irish arts organisations planning to engage in fundraising activities may have difficulty in building the necessary fundraising skills or in sourcing suitable candidates for recruitment.

---

[2] *Ibid.*

[3] Donoghue, F. *et al.*, *Exploring the Irish Fundraising Landscape: A report on the practice and scale of charitable fundraising from the Republic of Ireland* (Irish Charities Tax Research Limited; Centre for Nonprofit Management, School of Business, Trinity College Dublin, 2007).

[4] *Ibid.*

[5] *Ibid.*

[6] McGee, S. and Donoghue, F., "The Conundrum of Fundraising in Nonprofit Organisations: A Story from Ireland" (2009) Vol. 21, Issue 4, *Journal of Nonprofit & Public Sector Marketing*, 367–83.

[7] *Ibid.*

[8] *Ibid.*

[9] *Ibid.*

Donors and Donees

The link between donors and the organisations they fund, and the appropriateness of certain donors giving to certain organisations – given the values and activities of both parties – is a largely unresearched area in Ireland. Irish research on donors and donations in general is as yet sparse, reflecting the lack of sophistication in this market. A 'typology' of donors and donations, using stakeholder theory, has been developed in Canada by Paul Dunn. In his article "Strategic Responses by a Nonprofit when a Donor becomes Tainted", Dunn discusses the incongruence that occurs when the values and activities of a non-profit are inconsistent with those of a donor.[10] He shows how the stakeholder theory of Mitchell *et al.* can be applied to the non-profit sector,[11] i.e. when the claims of a stakeholder have legitimacy, power and urgency:

> "Management must attend to and give priority to that stakeholder's claim. The combination of these three attributes gives salience to the claim by the stakeholder and it gives the stakeholder considerable influence upon the organisation."[12]

Dunn contends that there should be a matching of donor and 'donee' (i.e. the fundraising organisation), and that the relationship is symmetrical: though the donor decides to give funds to an organisation whose values are synchronous with the donor's values and goals, the receiving organisation must also agree to receive the donation. In our context, the receiving arts organisation must therefore be satisfied that accepting a donation does not compromise its values and goals. If the donor "becomes tainted" as per Paul Dunn's definition, then the arts organisation will need to "get out of the deal", or break links with the donor. For example, if an arts organisation discovers that one of its donors is giving it funds generated from illegal activities, the arts organisation will want to reject the donation. These considerations are as relevant for those managing corporate governance and risk in an arts organisation as they are for its fundraisers.

---

[10] Dunn, P., "Strategic Responses by a Nonprofit when a Donor becomes Tainted" (2010) Vol. 39, No. 1, *Nonprofit and Voluntary Sector Quarterly*, 102–23.

[11] Mitchell, R. *et al.*, "Toward a Theory of Stakeholder Identification and Salience: Defining the Principle of Who and What Really Counts" (1997) Vol. 22, No. 4, *Academy of Management Review*, 853–86.

[12] *Ibid.*

Funders as Drivers of Good Corporate Governance

Against the backdrop of funding changes and its governance implications, funders are the main drivers of good governance in the sector, since they insist on demonstrable compliance with a stated code or framework prior to the giving of grants (this is justifiable from a funder's viewpoint, as they in turn are accountable, e.g. to the taxpayer, a philanthropist, etc.). However, from an arts organisation's viewpoint, the burden of compliance with governance requirements must not outweigh or stifle the creativity needed to produce great art. As discussed, this is a fine balance, the importance of which is unique to this sector.

Meanwhile, arts organisations tend to recognise the need for good corporate governance, but they tend to do so for expedience, to satisfy legal compliance and funder requirements. While interviews with representatives from the Irish arts sector supported the view that organisations seeking grants do comply with governance requirements, one interviewee revealed that some of their grant beneficiaries see fundraising as "a necessary evil", and governance as "almost secondary".

As discussed in **Chapter 3**, broad guidelines for corporate governance can be found in legislation and in codes of best practice, such as the *UK Corporate Governance Code*. Non-profit organisations, of which arts organisations are a subset, have a further refinement of governance structures as identified in the Charities Act 2009 and in the *Governance Code for Community, Voluntary and Charitable Organisations*.[13] It is important for arts organisations to customise their governance framework to suit their particular needs and to use it well.

Funding organisations are always anxious to see that their funds are being wisely spent. This particularly applies to funding organisations dispensing taxpayer money, such as the Arts Council or city and county councils. These organisations will make great efforts to drive accountability in the organisations they are funding in order to show that the funds are being properly spent. For these funders, grant documentation often stipulates that conditions must be met before money is granted.

Arts organisations sometimes complain about being rejected by funders or having their annual grants cut; but the funders are also accountable to those who ultimately supply the money. In the case of the Arts Council, city and county councils and European funding organisations, the money is coming from the taxpayer. Ultimately, these funders are publicly accountable.

---

[13] www.governancecode.ie.

Corporate Governance, Transparency and the Giving of Grants

Corporate governance in Irish arts organisations has been driven primarily by funders and grant givers, and standards have been uneven. Funders and beneficiaries interviewed were clear that the funders' demands for transparency and accountability are what currently drive corporate governance in the sector.

There is evidence that arts organisations identify a link between corporate governance and successful fundraising. Major philanthropic organisations will not give large grants ('large' being approximately €1 million to €5 million) unless a detailed review of the prospective beneficiary and its governance takes place. And funders require real evidence of good governance, transparency, clear financial statements and the overall effectiveness of the organisation.

In general, visibility and transparency in the Irish arts sector are lacking. Of even greater concern is that the sector does not seem to realise how important these attributes are as prerequisites for funding. While funders do seek and value artistic merit, they will first want to ensure that their funds will be used well and appropriately by the organisation. It is therefore important for the sector to be aware that implementing and demonstrating good governance will align artistic objectives with structures that will ensure their success and sustainability.

Funding Institutions' Expectations of Governance in Arts Organisations

The Arts Council is the largest grant giver in the Irish arts sector. An analysis of its awards in 2012 shows that 82% of its award monies were granted to organisations rather than to individuals (this figure was 83% in 2011). Therefore, the criteria and frameworks for good corporate governance apply to most of the Arts Council's grant-giving activities. (These figures are detailed in charts in **Appendix 11**.)

The expectation of good governance in arts organisations is well evidenced in the requirements of grant application forms. A short review of the conditions to be fulfilled for the receipt of a grant from major funders of the sector is provided in **Appendix 8**. In this review of the funding criteria, it is clear that the funding conditions increase with the size of the grant. The criteria vary from the production of audited accounts to permission for the funder to attend board meetings. It also shows the expectation of being a properly constituted company, a bank account, frequent board meetings, up-to-date tax affairs and frequent reporting to the grant-giver.

The Monitoring of Funded Organisations

Not surprisingly, funders monitor the organisations they fund. For example, the monitoring by the Arts Council and the Ireland Funds is in two forms. First, there is monitoring of the proper use of the grant (this can include a governance review); secondly, the Arts Council carries out artistic monitoring, and the Ireland Funds carry out project visits (these can be a form of artistic quality assurance).

The monitoring depends on the size of the grant given. Funders tend to be constrained by the costs of monitoring and reviewing good governance in funded organisations. This is appropriate, as undue monitoring of small organisations would be too expensive and intrusive. This observation suggests that governance is being driven by the funders, rather than by the arts organisations. Governance is still being imposed on arts organisations through the compliance requirements for grant receipt. Thus, instead of governance being driven downwards from the board, it is being driven upwards from the grant proposals. This fragments governance in the sector as a whole and makes governance standards uneven.

There was agreement amongst interviewees and clients that there is no causal link between good corporate governance and good art. The monitoring of grants follows the grant money or separately assesses the artistic output. This book identifies corporate governance as an enabler for well-run arts organisations.

Transparency and Balance

Interestingly, towards the end of my interviews, asked if there were any other issues they would like to discuss, the representatives from the arts sector unanimously pointed to the costs and benefits of governance, with concerns about the risk of over-governance.

All were clear on the need for balance. There is a concern amongst funders that arts organisations need to turn corporate governance accountability and transparency into a dynamic opportunity rather than a chore, and this can be a considerable challenge for small organisations often burdened by administration. Discussing the costs of raising funds efficiently in the sector, it was said of the Charities Act: "The opportunity for transparency and accountability is an opportunity to come clean for us, to run the sector, and to attract people into this sector." Similarly, the website of the Department of Community, Equality and Gaeltacht Affairs declares that the Charities Act "will also enhance public trust and confidence in charities and increase transparency in the sector."[14]

The balance between creativity and artistry and the need for good governance is one the arts sector feels it needs to continuously communicate. Warnings such as, "If we ever reached a stage where we insist on corporate governance before artistry, then we have lost out", were normal during interviews. Arts organisations are clear that they need to ensure that corporate governance is not a dead hand on innovation and creativity, that it should be an enabler of artistic endeavour.

For Irish arts organisations, artistic merit must be the priority and it is important that this priority is never lost. At the conclusion of my interviews, it was interesting to note that the interviewees, while respecting the need for governance, were clear that artistic merit is to be the driver of well-governed organisations. As one interviewee said succinctly: "The idea has to come first … If good corporate governance follows, this means that it is a magic mix."

The pursuit of the 'magic mix' is what this book is about. The balance between artistry and effective financial support for our cultural organisations will make our society a better place, driven by a resounding, inclusive and excellent cultural agenda.

Large and Small Arts Organisations and Fundraising

The fundraising sector in Ireland is underdeveloped, partly because Irish tax credits for charitable giving are less than those in, for example, the US and partly because of a lack of policy in the area. The current shortage of funds and the arrival of new legislation mean it is a good time to address this lack of documented policy.

Larger arts organisations realise that good corporate governance is a prerequisite for being granted funding from external sources, but this is largely untrue for smaller arts organisations. Interviewees from the larger, regularly funded organisations were clearly aware of the Arts Council's

[14] Department of Community, Equality and Gaeltacht Affairs (www.pobail.ie, accessed 24 July 2011).

governance requirements. In these cases, good governance is being driven by funders, which in many cases is the Arts Council.

A review of the grant application forms of selected grant givers in the Irish arts sector (see **Appendix 8)** shows how the disclosure requirements of funded organisations tend to increase with the size of the grant. As discussed, the larger the amount involved, the more rigorous the review process carried out by the funders. For funders who are dispensing taxpayer money, this approach is logical – the more money being given, the more conditions will be attached to ensure that the money is safe.

The scenario is different for small organisations and for smaller grant amounts. McGee and Donoghue identify "considerable informality in the sector",[15] which is supported by my interviews with representatives from the Irish arts sector, who pointed to the need to educate, raise awareness and, for small organisations, to be more realistic in terms of the amount of money they ask for and the viability of their projects. Considering the size of arts organisations ("55% of participating arts organisations have less than five employees"[16]), this result is consistent.

However, it must be concluded that where the management response of arts organisations is compliant rather than collaborative, it is clearly the funders who are driving corporate governance standards.

For many arts organisations the Arts Council is their sole funder. Though funding from sources outside Ireland is available, it is rarely sought; for example, in my research I found only one organisation that had made itself ready to receive tax-deductible contributions from the US. (This involved applying for and receiving charitable classification through the completion of the 501(c)(3) form issued by the US Internal Revenue Service.)

Summary

In researching this study of governance issues in the Irish arts sector, my sources ranged from business reports and academic writing to the opinions and advice of professionals. Expertise was sought not only from the arts

---

[15] McGee, S. and Donoghue, F., "The Conundrum of Fundraising in Nonprofit Organisations: A Story from Ireland" (2009) Vol. 21, Issue 4, *Journal of Nonprofit & Public Sector Marketing*, 367–83.

[16] Business to Arts, *Private Investment in Arts and Culture: Survey Report* (conducted by Deloitte, 2008).

sector but also corporate governance and accounting professionals from the non-profit sector whose experience spanned Ireland, the United States and beyond.

The arts will not get funding if they do not or cannot show good governance. The lack of awareness of the benefits of corporate governance for the sector indicates a need for training, education, publication and coordination of governance efforts in the sector.

Then, when it is embraced and introduced, the governance framework needs to be scaled according to size and complexity of the organisation. The governance framework needs to facilitate clear standards against which organisations can measure themselves. The adoption of agreed accounting standards, as discussed by Teresa Harrington in *Accounting and Reporting by Charities in the Republic of Ireland*, would facilitate uniform and comparable accounting in the sector.

That governance is being driven by the funders is an important finding. It suggests that grant-giving should carry stipulations about corporate governance and that procedures should be in place to ensure that no monies are given without evidence that funders' requirements of governance, financial reporting and internal controls are being met. It also highlights the need for training and for financial expertise in the arts sector. These measures will be necessary to ensure the sustainability and continuance of our arts organisations.

The funding landscape is changing and recent initiatives are making fundraising practices a necessary part of Irish arts organisations' activities. Within and on behalf of arts organisations, fundraising practices are underdeveloped and it is difficult to find sophisticated, professional fundraisers in Ireland, which is related to the fact that ours is a grant-giving rather than a fundraising culture – organisations that are funded by grants do not generally need to fundraise.

Chapter 9

Looking Forward

Trust and integrity play an essential role in economic life and for the sake of business and future prosperity we have to make sure that they are properly rewarded.

OECD (2004)

Introduction

Demands are increasing for corporate governance to become embedded in business and business processes. Organisations are encouraged to include in their published annual reports at least a paragraph about how corporate governance is conducted and what governance processes are used in the organisation. New governance-related legislation and draft legislation proliferate, and businesses all over the world are being urged to improve diversity on boards, embody ethical business practices and implement better controls. (The Sarbanes–Oxley legislation in the USA is an example: section 404 of the Sarbanes–Oxley Act requires US-listed companies to file a report of management assessment of internal controls operating in the company in the financial year.) The future will see greater and more visible demand for compliance with corporate governance standards and best practice, as well as increased visibility of corporate governance practices within organisations, such as board rotation, executive salary disclosure, boardroom organisation and public accountability.

In Irish arts organisations, the trends outlined above are intensified for those which receive funding from public sources. In those organisations, governance standards are increasingly required to be very transparent, as they are under continuous scrutiny.

We have seen how the business models and funding models are shifting in response to a shortage of funds. The Arts Council, the largest funder, has itself suffered funding cuts from the State. This has meant that our arts organisations are required to shift from a model of single-source funding to a model that demands fundraising and multiple funding sources. The arm's-length, peer-reviewed model of funding does bring about a form of democracy for the funding of good art. We have seen that the alternative can mean that funding comes from wealthy individuals or a politically biased government. Where the former can be slow and contentious, the latter can be unduly influenced by the political inclinations of the direct funders. If we move from arm's-length funding from an independent Arts Council to a more mixed model which includes direct philanthropy, that 'mixed funding' model will have implications for the art our society produces.

This mixed funding model will have mixed consequences. Stakeholder theory suggests that the board and executive management treat funders as stakeholders and that a key role of the board will be to balance stakeholder needs. Such an identification of the increased importance of stakeholders will move Irish arts organisations closer to the model where funders of the arts organisations will become more important and the role of the board will include fulfilling the needs and expectations of the stakeholders. (A comparison of the theoretical perspectives of organisational governance is provided in **Appendix 10**, where the stakeholder model identifies "balancing stakeholder needs" as a primary role of the board.) In future, arts organisations will need to be fully compliant and transparent in relation to their corporate governance practices as stakeholders demand accountability through increased corporate governance.

If we move towards a more mixed model of funding the arts, fundraising is also likely to become an integral part of arts organisations and fundraisers are likely to change the funding landscape. These fundraisers will inevitably establish schemes by which members of the public can fund their favourite arts organisations and receive some reward in kind for doing so. Fund it, Kickstarter and Linked Finance are some recent examples of ways to seek direct funding from the public. Fund it states that it is "an Ireland-wide initiative that provides a platform for people with great ideas to attract funding from friends, fans and followers across the world".[1] Many small arts organisations are using Fund it to great effect: Macnas, an award-winning theatre, spectacle and processional company, used Fund it to fund its activities in 2013. This type of direct, online fundraising is becoming more common.

Pressure may also grow to allow donations to non-profit organisations to have some form of tax allowance attached, and this will further increase requirements for those non-profit organisations to be transparent and demonstrably well-governed.

---

[1] www.fundit.ie (accessed 10 May 2014).

Increased fundraising activities will also require additional disclosure in arts organisations' financial statements (this has been addressed by the Charities Act 2009). It now seems likely that some further implementation of the Charities Act is being undertaken by the current Government and at the time of writing (September 2014), a charities regulator has recently been appointed and has commenced setting up an Office of the Charities Regulator. The present Act called for a Charities Regulation Authority[2] to be established, and this move was welcomed by the sector.

However, accounting practitioners have noted that the current Charities Act does not require charities to apply the Statement of Recommended Practice (SORP).[3] If the Act were to provide a standard recommended format for charities' accounting, it would make the financial statements of charities transparent and comparable. The current ongoing consultation process between government and charitable organisations may produce some interest in a recommended accounting practice for the financial statements of Irish charities. For many arts organisations that are registered as charities, this would mean they would have to comply with the recommended accounting formats.

Arts organisations that fundraise and have not yet adopted the recommendations of the SORP will likely need to make changes to the formats of their financial statements. Arts organisations that do not fundraise are less likely to need significant changes to their financial statements, as has been discussed by Teresa Harrington in *Accounting and Reporting by Charities in the Republic of Ireland*.[4] Although the Charities Act will be very important for the element of the sector that are registered charities, ultimately the boards of these organisations will need to drive the changes from within.

Arts Boards

Governance comes from the board and there is currently an increasing focus on the effectiveness and operation of arts boards. Ireland is no stranger to the criticism levelled by the Canadian writer Johanne Turbide:

---

[2] The Department of Justice and Equality appointed Úna Ní Dhubhghaill to commence the implementation of the Charities Act Regulation Authority in Dublin. Reported on www.charteredaccountants.ie (accessed 28 January 2013).

[3] The Statement of Recommended Practice is mandatory in the UK and viewed as best practice in Ireland.

[4] Harrington, T., *Accounting and Reporting by Charities in the Republic of Ireland* (Chartered Accountants Ireland, 2011).

"Conversely, in cases of organisational or financial difficulty, we are quick to point the finger at board members: 'Who are these people? Were they asleep? Why did they allow the executive director and his or her team to make such risky decisions?' With remarkable ease, we assign criticism and blame to the board members: 'The board was irresponsible. It governed badly!'"[5]

In difficult financial times, much is expected of arts boards. The need for clear, visible and comprehensive board documents and policies is more important than ever, and I have referred throughout this book to codes of corporate governance appropriate for use by Irish arts organisations of different sizes.

Although I have found instances of lack of awareness of good governance in all types of arts organisations, generally boards are aware that good governance and accountability is being driven by the funders. Furthermore, the current need for fundraising will probably drive an improvement in corporate governance standards. This requires arts organisations to be aware of corporate governance, what it means and how to embody it. It requires arts organisations to make the link between fundraising or receiving funds from grant-givers and demonstrating that they are well governed.

Arts organisations do show a better level of diversity on their boards than Irish public limited companies. An important aspect of good governance is skills diversity on the board (and always a necessity on arts boards); boards that include diverse skills of not only artistic input but of financial, legal and other skills will fare better. EU studies show that the presence of diverse skills and thinking improves board performance. Although there is a lack of data for this important aspect of diversity on Irish arts boards, the future is clamouring for diversity.[6] It is likely that our non-profit boards could lead the way, if the sector gives due importance to the diversity of its boards.

Challenges for the Future

There is a challenge for organisations in the sector to coordinate more with each other. The arts sector is made up of a large number of small organisations,

---

[5] Turbide, J., "Can Good Governance Prevent Financial Crises in Arts Organizations?" (2012) Vol. 14, No. 2, *International Journal of Arts Management*, 4–16.

[6] In 2012, EC Vice President Viviane Reding announced that the European Commission was considering the imposition of quotas to improve gender balance on the boards of listed European companies.

often with the same or a similar purpose, operating in the same geographical area, often subscribing to the same representative organisation or umbrella group. Many of these organisations, including the representative groups, look to the same sources for funding. While healthy competition is reassuring, and value for money is being achieved, more rationalisation could lead to greater efficiency, professionalism, and a more powerful and purposeful sector.

For companies without share capital and limited by guarantee, mergers and rationalisations are less obvious and straightforward than mergers and takeovers among companies with share capital, and it is likely that the drive for greater coordination will be driven by the funders and stakeholders. Furthermore, companies without share capital and limited by guarantee are not driven by a profit motive – they operate on the basis of breaking even and spending funds available to them in the financial year. Without that profit motive, these organisations need to identify other criteria or drivers for any potential mergers or collaborations, and these will usually be on the basis of collaboration around the running of a specific event or festival to fulfil their cultural objectives.

However, mergers may not always be the best course of action. While merger and greater scale may increase influence of the arts organisations and their ability to fundraise, it could also reduce the diversity of ideas and the number of initiatives coming from the sector.

Developing Ethical Standards

Recent debate on salaries and remuneration in the non-profit and public sectors has caused anger and confusion.[7] The transparency around costs, expenses and employee remuneration has led to loud debate on transparency in the sector and how to benchmark reasonable remuneration. Damage has also been done to the not-for-profit sector as a whole,[8] which has emphasised the need for a Charities Regulator (who was appointed in March 2014).

There is a tendency for the media and the public to call for investigation into the governance of organisations on the basis that there is 'no smoke without fire', which brings more problems. We have seen that when one organisation

---

[7] O'Brien, C. and Wall, M., "Chief executive of Central Remedial Clinic resigns", *The Irish Times*, 22 April 2014.

[8] O'Sullivan, C., "Charity donations down 40% after CRC scandal", *Irish Examiner*, 25 January 2014.

in the non-profit sector behaves unethically, all similar organisations come under the same scrutiny.

The values of boards and of CEOs are being questioned. There is also increasing emphasis on ethical standards as the conversation on governance moves to discussions of accountability and, inevitably, to the actions of the board and individual board directors, whose values will permeate the organisation.

Recent scandals relating to the roles of the boards of banks in the economic crisis, which started in 2008, have amplified the volume of calls for more responsible and ethical boards. The taxpaying public also want the values of individual board members to be based on ethical standards and to know what exactly those ethics are; any evidence of personal greed, lack of integrity, lack of appropriate qualification or lack of transparency is being highlighted in the media.

Manuel G. Velasquez, in his book *Business Ethics: Concepts and Cases*, defines ethics as "The discipline that examines one's moral standards".[9] Velasquez goes on to discuss business ethics, which he defines as "a specialised study of moral right and wrong that concentrates on moral standards as they apply to business institutions, organisations, and behaviour." If this is the case, good corporate governance suggests that boards must consider basic ethical standards as part of their corporate governance requirements. Establishing an effective board must include the consideration of conflicts of interest and the integrity of directors. Most governance scandals emanate from the board, and often from its alleged misconduct. From the definition provided by Velasquez above, we can say that ethics are about moral decisions. Ethical behaviour by board members is therefore 'moral' behaviour.

Dr Patricia Barker places ethics firmly within one's individual values: "Our exasperation with regulation should not give us an excuse for failing to come to grips with the real underpinning reason for corporate collapse – the failure of individuals to apply strong personal ethical values."[10] If ethics on a board are about personal ethical values, then the careful selection and recruitment of board members becomes very important. Board members should display values similar to those of the organisation, as their recruitment will influence the values and culture of that organisation.

[9] Velasquez, M.G., *Business Ethics: Concepts and Cases* (7th edition) (Pearson, 2014).
[10] Barker, P., "Ethics Fatigue – Regulation vs Integrity", *Accountancy Ireland*, October 2006.

The growing social demand for more ethical business practices from organisations will prove influential:

> "A fundamental truth is that business cannot exist without society and that society cannot go forward without business. Thus, business must acknowledge society's existence and society's growing demand for more ethically responsible business practice."[11]

For boards of directors and their corporate governance, this has two implications. First, the board must consider society's demands for ethical practices; and secondly, the board must increasingly consider the moral and ethical values of its directors. It must therefore seek to recruit directors with ethical values that are similar to its own. Conversely, prospective directors should consider the same question. This finding was echoed by one interviewee, who recommended that prospective board members look at the values of a board before accepting a position on it. With the current interest in directors' liabilities and responsibilities, it is becoming more important for prospective directors to ensure that the values of the prospective organisation are not at odds with their own values and business ethics. Instances of directors resigning from boards due to conflicts in values and judgements reflect badly on all parties concerned.

Values and Ethics – Organisational Ethics

As discussed in **Chapter 4**, arts organisations often measure themselves by their values rather than financial performance. Many arts organisations are created and sustained by the passionately held values of their founders and stakeholders. A prerequisite for any board is a reasonable interest in the organisational values on the part its members. Regardless of skills and qualifications, a passion and interest in what the organisation is trying to achieve is a foundation for the growth and development of a cohesive and effective board, and it is a requirement for a useful and contributing board member.

As discussed above, good corporate governance involves and demands the alignment of the values of individual board directors with the organisation's values, as one influences the other. Irial O'Farrell defines organisational or company values as follows: "Company values represent the company's internal set of standards it expects everyone within the organisation, including

---

[11] Joyner, B. and Payne, D., "Evolution and Implementation: A Study of Values, Business Ethics and Corporate Social Responsibility" (2002) Vol. 41, *Journal of Business Ethics*, 297–311.

the executive team, to live up to. They embody the business approach to achieving its purpose."[12] It is hoped that organisations' ethical values will be identified and rewarded in the future, as writers such as Manuel Velasquez argue that "habitually unethical behaviour is not necessarily a good long term business strategy for the company".[13]

The OECD also asks that integrity in business be rewarded: "Trust and integrity play an essential role in economic life and for the sake of business and future prosperity, we have to make sure that they are properly rewarded."[14]

Corporate Social Responsibility and Organisational Values

Ethics and corporate social responsibility (CSR) are interdependent:

> "These concepts of values, ethics/morality and CSR are not mutually exclusive; rather, they are interrelated and somewhat interdependent. Values influence the extent of a corporation's perceived social responsibility and are influenced by societal activities and norms or standards."[15]

For many non-profit arts organisations, CSR can involve coordination with companies willing to fund arts activities. Arts organisations are generally in receipt of CSR initiatives by for-profit organisations. Business in the Community Ireland (BITCI) is an organisation that fosters such CSR programmes. Its mission is "to harness the power of Irish business to maximise its positive impact on all its stakeholders and society".[16] Corporate governance within an arts organisation will need to be visible for CSR partners. The ethical issues around the values of funders and arts organisations have been examined above, identifying the "incongruence that occurs when the values and activities of a nonprofit are inconsistent with the values and activities of a donor".[17] For arts organisations that are becoming more involved in diverse fundraising, the values and ethical standards of coordinating CSR

---

[12] O'Farrell, I., *Values – Not Just for the Office Wall Plaque: How Personal and Company Values Intersect* (Evolution Consulting, 2012).

[13] Velasquez, M.G., *Business Ethics: Concepts and Cases* (7th edition) (Pearson, 2014).

[14] *Principles of Corporate Governance* (OECD Publications Service, 2004).

[15] Joyner, B. and Payne, D., "Evolution and Implementation: A Study of Values, Business Ethics and Corporate Social Responsibility" (2002) Vol. 41, *Journal of Business Ethics*, 297–311.

[16] www.bitc.ie (accessed January 2014).

[17] Dunn, P., "Strategic Responses by a Nonprofit when a Donor becomes Tainted" (2010) Vol. 39, No. 1, *Nonprofit and Voluntary Sector Quarterly*, 102–23.

initiatives and of responsibly contributing to the community will derive from their own mission, ethics and values.

Arts organisations make very suitable partners for for-profit organisations wishing to further their CSR programmes. The Irish organisation Business to Arts has organised interesting partnerships between arts organisations and large, for-profit companies. Arts organisations themselves are also good at coordinating CSR initiatives in collaboration with for-profit organisations. For example, Business to Arts collaborates with insurance company Allianz to hold the Allianz Business to Arts Awards. Business to Arts showcases the success and creativity of partnerships in achieving both the business's and arts organisation's (or artist's) objectives. Each award recipient is an example of best practice at building and sustaining partnerships that contribute to the aims and objectives of the artist or arts organisation and the for-profit business with which is collaborates.

The greater involvement of arts organisations in CSR partnerships will highlight the potential of such initiatives to the sector at large – this will also lead to a greater appreciation of the sector's own social responsibilities. These initiatives are likely to be driven by fundraising work by arts organisations, which will inevitably include for-profit organisations. Hopefully, they will broaden the bridge of understanding between the arts and business sectors.

Organisational Structures and the Companies Bill 2012

New companies legislation in Ireland will affect arts organisations, how they are structured and governed. Though not yet enacted at the time of writing, some of the changes likely to be introduced by the new Companies Bill are as follows:[18]

- It will be easier to set up a limited company.
- It will not be necessary to hold a meeting for the AGM – this can be done in writing.
- The responsibilities and duties of directors will be simplified.

The Bill also provides for the creation of a DAC (designated activity company) limited by guarantee, which will replace the current form of company limited

[18] Quinlan, P. and Millar, E., "Companies Bill 2012" (2013) Vol. 45, No. 1, *Accountancy Ireland.*

by guarantee common among arts organisations. DACs can have up to 149 members and a minimum of two directors. The memorandum and articles of association that are currently required will be replaced by one document for the constitution of the DAC.

The implications of this for Irish arts organisations could be very positive. The new Companies Bill should simplify compliance for small organisations struggling with companies legislation. Part of the Bill is designed specifically to simplify compliance for guarantee companies limited by guarantee (CLGs). As discussed in **Chapter 1**, the majority of arts organisations are CLGs.

Summary

Corporate governance is one of the most widely discussed business topics at present. As the world attempts to move on from recession, we are learning from its harsh experiences. In many of the largest financial scandals, it has been observed that corporate governance was lacking. Throughout all organisations there is concern about compliance with governance best practice. As the arts sector shifts to more diverse funding models in more competitive funding environments, it is showing increasing concern with the implementation and demonstration of good corporate governance.

Meanwhile, the discipline of corporate governance becomes ever more fine-tuned, with the introduction and adoption of new standards and guidelines for arts organisations. Non-profits are now shifting to a more sophisticated governance model, addressing transparency, accountability, ethical standards, board diversity and improved financial reporting. Statements of governance standards are more frequently being disclosed in financial statements. However, corporate governance is about principles, not just rules, and it depends highly on the effectiveness, ethics and values of the board.

We have seen how corporate governance is valuable as an enabler for excellence in arts organisations. With good and visible corporate governance, arts organisations can become more accountable, more transparent and more fundable.

Just as businesspeople can appropriate artistic practices to enhance their profession, artists can appropriate business practices to enhance theirs. Both professions have much to learn from each other, and much to gain from collaboration. Artists talk of associative rather than linear thinking, understanding the imaginative leaps that can come from a creative mind. Business practices call this 'innovation' or 'jumping the curve'.[19]

What of the future of corporate governance in the arts sector? Discussions around ethical values and standards, and the standards of boards, will shift the focus to board selection processes and the recruitment of suitable board members. This discussion is being fuelled by reports from the EU and the US exhorting diversity on boards and praising the benefits of diverse thinking – not just so that boards can represent the communities they are supposed to be serving but also so that their collective decisions can be made better by the inclusion of many viewpoints.

With regard to the 'stakeholders' in arts organisations, the debate is well underway to identify those communities which organisations are supposed to be serving. We discussed stakeholders in **Chapter 2** as those "groups and individuals who have a stake in the success or failure of a business", and such definitions and theories may inform this debate.[20]

The concept of 'stewardship' and related guidance may also be of value to the governance of the arts. On stewardship by institutional investors in large public companies, the essence of the FRC's guidance[21] involves the responsibilities of institutional investors to the businesses in which they invest. Stewardship activities include monitoring and engaging with companies on matters such as strategy, performance, risk, capital structure and corporate governance, including culture and remuneration. Engagement is purposeful dialogue with companies on those matters as well as on issues that are the immediate subject of votes at general meetings. This guidance establishes a reflexive relationship or a shared responsibility on the part of the stakeholder and the organisation in which they have invested.

[19] The phrase used here, "jumping the curve", comes from: Imparato, N. and Harari, O., *Jumping the Curve: Innovation and Strategic Choice in an Age of Transition* (Jossey Bass Publishers, 1996). Elliot W. Eisner in *The Arts and the Creation of Mind* (Yale University Press, 2002) discusses the importance of art in education and its use as a lever for learning and understanding. Peter Senge in *The Dance of Change* (Doubleday, 1999) identifies command and control mechanisms of governance in organisations and compares them to directing and adjusting systems, where interdependences are recognised. He discusses the conditions for change and transformation in organisations from a charodic or disruptive/collaborative process, thus making the link between business processes and innovation through a non-linear thinking process. This is a place which the arts understand so well as an integral part of their creative process.

[20] Freeman, R. *et al.*, *Stakeholder Theory: The State of the Art* (Cambridge University Press, 2010).

[21] Financial Reporting Council, *The UK Stewardship Code* (2012).

In terms of the corporate governance of arts organisations, this thinking suggests that the future will require stakeholders or investors to engage with organisations in more meaningful ways. No longer will it be adequate to fund arts organisations with public monies; those funders will be required to engage with the organisation and its values, strategy and culture. This will create a more unified arts sector, with stakeholders enabled and empowered to engage with arts organisations.

Chapter 10

Final Words

It has been such a pleasure to work in the arts and cultural sector. I continue to work with the conviction that the arts and business sectors not only can collaborate with each other but can learn from each other's thinking and work practices. Certainly, this study has led to the conclusion that corporate governance is necessary, even for small companies. It is especially necessary in a sector that receives funding from public funds.

Public funding demands accountability and, in particular, transparency. Recent scandals have made it clear that funders and taxpayers lose confidence in the whole sector when there is any lack of transparency.

Many talented and creative people work in the arts sector, and this book shows that the introduction and implementation of corporate governance best practice, codes and standards work as an enabler for these good people; it is through good governance that they will secure the funding for their organisations.

Most Irish arts organisations are small by global standards and the level of corporate governance sophistication necessary for these organisations can be low and their governance standards basic. Nevertheless, as this book has shown, exactly the same *principles* of governance apply; it is only their implementation that varies. Also, more and more the Irish public are demanding higher standards of governance and accountability and this is clearly demonstrated by the vociferous reactions to any improprieties or wastage of monies within the funded sectors.[1]

While this book has discussed the 'arts sector', it remains difficult to quantify and define it. There is, however, an ongoing need for a quantification of the arts sector in Ireland. The work of the Centre for Nonprofit Management at Trinity College Dublin has helped identify the non-profit sector in Ireland, and within that research some figures are available for the arts sector. It is tempting to reorganise and reanalyse these figures to provide estimates of the arts sector, but the validity of the estimates would

---

[1] There was major public outcry in early 2014 in relation to monies paid covertly to an executive of the Central Remedial Clinic in Dublin.

be questionable, as the primary research is designed for the non-profit sector as a whole.

What *is* known is that larger arts organisations are different from small arts organisations and that there are between 350 and 1,477 arts organisations in Ireland.[2] Some are funded by the Arts Council, some are unfunded, and the standards and awareness of governance in these organisations can vary. Research based on the size of organisations would be helpful for policy-makers to identify the educational and funding needs of these organisations in order to ensure their sustainability.

Due to variations in tax credits and government grants available, funding in the arts sectors differs between countries and the drivers of good corporate governance may differ as well. Comparisons of best practices could be made to provide benchmarking and improved frameworks in the Irish sector. The appointment of Ms Úna Ní Dhubhghaill as the chief executive of the new Charities Regulatory Authority will perhaps enable these issues to be addressed.

The future is bright for the arts sector – it experienced growth in the boom years, and although funding cuts have been deep and severe, they have not been proportionate to cuts endured in other sectors during the recession. There is a growing interest in the arts and, importantly, to what the arts might contribute to thinking that could pull the world out of cyclical recessions and into a more sustainable model.

In January 2013, the Arts in Education Charter agreement between the Minister for Arts, Heritage and the Gaeltacht and the Minister for Education and Skills recognised the role of the arts in Irish education, and there is a growing interest in how the arts can be an agent of change in modern society. The works of authors such as Elliot Eisner,[3] Howard Gardner[4] and Mihaly Csikszentmihalyi[5] are examples of studies on creativity and how it can be appropriated by other disciplines.

Can the arts show us the way to move forward from postmodernism, which arguably sowed the seeds for recession in its consumerist, mass-media-defined

---

[2] Donoghue *et al.*, *The Hidden Landscape: First Forays into Mapping Nonprofit Organisations in Ireland* (Centre for Nonprofit Management, School of Business, Trinity College Dublin, 2006).

[3] Eisner, E., *The Arts and the Creation of Mind* (Yale University Press, 2002).

[4] Gardner, H.E., *Multiple Intelligences: New Horizons in Theory and Practice* (Basic Books, 2006).

[5] Csikszentmihalyi, M., *Finding Flow: The Psychology of Engagement with Everyday Life* (Basic Books, 1998).

culture and its rejection of modernist 'grand narratives', allowing the acceleration of the rollercoaster of boom and recession in the economic marketplaces? It would be game-changing for business to engage with the arts and to use the arts for "the making of meaning in modern society".[6]

Perhaps in the future we can "unlock the full potential of the critical and complex connection between culture, Ireland's international reputation, and business".[7]

---

[6] A phrase used by Declan McGonigle at a Theatre Forum conference in June 2013.
[7] Department of Foreign Affairs, "The Global Irish Economic Forum One Year On. A report on the follow up to the Global Irish Economic Forum at Farmleigh" (2010).

Appendix 1

Procedure for the Recruitment of New Board Members: Principles

The search for board candidates should be conducted, and appointments made, on merit, against objective criteria and with due regard for the benefits of diversity on the board, including gender. The board should satisfy itself that plans are in place for the orderly succession of board appointments and senior management. This will maintain an appropriate balance of skills and experience within the company and on the board and will ensure progressive, regular refreshing of the board.

The document below is reproduced courtesy of Cluid Housing Association.[1] It outlines a process for the recruitment of new board members.

1. Input by the full board should be sought in the recruitment of all new board members.
2. A needs analysis should be carried out by the board or a nomination committee, on an annual basis and in advance of the AGM. This is based on:
   • the number of board members currently needed;
   • skills, experience and competency gaps on the existing board; and
   • new skills/competencies which the board needs (referring to plans and strategies).
3. Having identified the skills required, the nomination committee presents its analysis to the board.
4. The board agrees the needs analysis. This can be reviewed as necessary, but in any event at the 'away day' when the available skill set can be assessed by the wider board.
5. Board members then suggest potential new board members to the board at the next meeting (they do not approach the potential candidates as no formal offer from the board is yet agreed). Potential conflicts of interest will be considered at this stage.
6. Board members add the suggested candidate names to the list.

---

[1] Cluid Housing Association (2012).

7. In addition, the board may, as appropriate, advertise and/or engage the services of outside recruiters to assist in the process of identifying suitable candidates.

8. The board considers, confidentially, the full list of candidates and this feedback is gathered by the chair in advance of meeting with the committee chairs.

9. Potential candidates will be considered by the chairs of the committees and the chair of the board. A shortlist will be drawn up and shortlisted candidates will then be invited to interview.

10. Interviews will be arranged and will be attended by the chair of the board and the chief executive or their nominated deputies.

11. This process of invitation continues until there is the quota of new board members to fill the skills gaps as defined.

12. Following a successful interview process, the chair will make a recommendation to the board regarding candidate appointment.

13. The board members will be invited to attend the next annual general meeting (AGM).

14. The new board members will be elected at the AGM.

Additional provisions from the *UK Corporate Governance Code* can also be included:

"Non-executive directors should be appointed for specified terms subject to re-election and to statutory provisions relating to the removal of a director. Any term beyond six years for a nonexecutive director should be subject to particularly rigorous review, and should take into account the need for progressive refreshing of the board."

"A separate section of the annual report should describe the work of the nomination committee, including the process it has used in relation to board appointments. This section should include a description of the board's policy on diversity, including gender, any measurable objectives that it has set for implementing the policy, and progress on achieving the objectives. An explanation should be given if neither an external search consultancy nor open advertising has been used in the appointment of a chairman or a non-executive director. Where an external search consultancy has been used, it should be identified in the annual report and a statement made as to whether it has any other connection with the company."

Appendix 2

Directors' Duties, Responsibilities and Liabilities in Financial Uncertainty[1]

Directors' Duties

Directors have a duty of care to the company of which they are a director. This means that they must act in the best interests of the company. In difficult financial circumstances, this can involve finding measures to keep the company solvent, such as close scrutiny of the company's financial affairs, cost-cutting, debt negotiation and/or the direction or organisation of additional fundraising activities.

Who are the Officers of the Company?

The officers of the company are the directors and the Company Secretary, and others who share legal liability for the actions of the company. These can include the chief executive officer (CEO) and chief financial officer (CFO).

Directors' Responsibilities

- Directors should take reasonable steps to ensure proper books of account are kept, and that an annual audit is carried out.
- Directors must ensure that annual returns are made to the Companies Registration Office.

---

[1] This factsheet was produced by the author for Theatre Forum Ireland, and is reproduced with the kind permission of Theatre Forum Ireland.

How do I Know if my Company is Insolvent?

There are two commonly used methods used to determine insolvency:

- The Cash Flow Test – can the company pay its debts (e.g. payroll and taxes) when they fall due?
- The Balance Sheet Test – are the company's assets greater than its liabilities? (e.g. do we owe more than others owe to us?)

If Your Company is in Financial Difficulty

There are a number of steps directors should take to improve the organisation's financial circumstances and to be able to defend themselves against possible charges of reckless trading.

- Convene more frequent board meetings, and encourage frequent meetings of the management team. Call an extraordinary general meeting (EGM) of members, if applicable.
- Take careful minutes and note down decisions taken, carefully noting the reasons and bases for the decisions. Ensure the minutes are complete and accurate and are carefully saved.
- Obtain financial advice, preferably from a qualified accountant.
- Prepare frequent management accounts to get a realistic picture of the company's state of affairs.
- Prepare a budget and a realistic business plan.
- It is better to hold early discussions with your bank and to keep them informed.
- For the largest creditors, keep them informed of your plans and, if necessary, negotiate payment plans with them. Only make promises that you can keep.
- If your organisation is insolvent, get insolvency advice from an insolvency practitioner or a qualified accountant.
- Discuss the situation with your auditors.

Directors' Liabilities

A director is guilty of reckless trading if, by continuing the business of the company, loss is caused to any of the company's creditors; or, if the director was a party to the contracting of a debt by the company and did not honestly believe on reasonable grounds that the company would be able to pay the debt when it fell due for payment as well as all its other debts. (Adapted from section 297A of the Companies Act 1963 as inserted by section 138 of the Companies Act 1990.)

In order to be found guilty of reckless trading, officers of the company must knowingly carry on the business of the company in a reckless manner. If reckless trading is proven, the directors, by order of the court, can be made personally liable (without limitation) for the company's debts from the time they knew the company was insolvent.

Winding Up

There are various ways of winding up a company. One common form is a members' voluntary liquidation, which is a form of winding up whereby the members decide, for commercial reasons, to wind up the company. In order to avail of this process the company is required to be solvent. Under this process, all creditor debts must be paid in full. It is advisable to seek the advice of your auditors or a qualified accountant if you intend to wind up your organisation.

Appendix 3

Principles from the *Code of Practice for Good Governance of Community, Voluntary and Charitable Organisations in Ireland* (2012) ('The Governance Code')

Principle 1. Leading our organisation. We do this by:
1. Agreeing our vision, purpose and values and making sure that they remain relevant.
2. Developing, resourcing, monitoring and evaluating a plan to make sure that our organisation achieves its stated purpose.
3. Managing, supporting and holding to account staff, volunteers and all who act on behalf of the organisation.

Principle 2. Exercising control over our organisation. We do this by:
1. Identifying and complying with all relevant legal and regulatory requirements.
2. Making sure that there are appropriate internal financial and management controls.
3. Identifying major risks for our organisation and deciding ways of managing those risks.

Principle 3. Being transparent and accountable. We do this by:
1. Identifying those who have a legitimate interest in the work of our organisation (stakeholders) and making sure that there is regular and effective communication with them about our organisation.
2. Responding to stakeholders' questions or views about the work of our organisation and how we run it.
3. Encouraging and enabling the engagement of those who benefit from our organisation in the planning and decision making of the organisation.

Principle 4. Working effectively. We do this by:

1. Making sure that our governing body, individual board members, committees, staff and volunteers understand their role, legal duties and delegated responsibility for decision-making.
2. Making sure that as a board we exercise our collective responsibility through board meetings that are efficient and effective.
3. Making sure that there is suitable board recruitment, development and retirement processes in place.

Principle 5. Behaving with integrity. We do this by:

1. Being honest, fair and independent.
2. Understanding, declaring and managing conflicts of interest and conflicts of loyalties.
3. Protecting and promoting our organisation's reputation.

Appendix 4

Share of Women on the Boards of the Largest Publicly Listed Companies in the EU (2010–2012)

	(% total board members)		
	2010 (Oct.)	2011 (Oct.)	2012 (Jan.)
EU-27	11.8	13.6	13.7
Belgium	10.5	10.9	10.7
Bulgaria	11.2	15.2	15.6
Czech Republic	12.2	15.9	15.4
Denmark	17.7	16.3	16.1
Germany	12.6	15.2	15.6
Estonia	7.0	6.7	6.7
Ireland	8.4	8.8	8.7
Greece	6.2	6.5	7.4
Spain	9.5	11.1	11.5
France	12.3	21.6	22.3
Italy	4.5	5.9	6.1
Cyprus	4.0	4.6	4.4
Latvia	23.5	26.6	25.9
Lithuania	13.1	14.0	14.5
Luxembourg	3.5	5.6	5.7
Hungary	13.6	5.3	5.3
Malta	2.4	2.3	3.0
Netherlands	14.9	17.8	18.5
Austria	8.7	11.1	11.2
Poland	11.6	11.8	11.8
Portugal	5.4	5.9	6.0
Romania	21.3	10.4	10.3
Slovenia	9.8	14.2	15.3
Slovakia	21.6	14.6	13.5

Finland	25.9	26.5	27.1
Sweden	26.4	24.7	25.2
United Kingdom	13.3	16.3	15.6

Source: European Commission database on women and men in decision making. (See http://ec.europa.eu)

Appendix 5

Excerpt from Charities Statement of Recommended Practice (FRS 102) (effective 1 January 2015)

Statement of financial activities

	Unre-stricted funds	Restricted funds	Endow-ment funds	Total funds	Prior period Total funds	Further details
	€/£	€/£	€/£	€/£	€/£	
Income and endowments from:						
Donations and legacies						A1
Charitable activities						A2
Other trading activities						A3
Investments						A4
Other						A5
Total						
Expenditure on:						
Raising funds						B1
Charitable activities						B2
Other						B3
Total						
Net gains/(losses) on investments						B4
Net income/ (expenditure)						
Transfers between funds						C
Other recognised gains/(losses):						

Gains/(losses) on revaluation of fixed assets						D1
Actuarial gains/(losses) on defined benefit pension schemes						D2
Other gains/(losses)						D3
Net movement in funds						
Reconciliation of funds:						E
Total funds brought forward						
Total funds carried forward						

Note: References in the 'Further details' column refer to sections in the SORP document, which is available at www.charitysorp.org.

Appendix 6

Corporate Governance Statements: Suggested Guidelines for the Content of a Statement in the Annual Report of an Arts Organisation[1]

- **Description of the key governance statement and document of the organisation**, e.g. the Memorandum and Articles of Association, Founding Charter, etc.
- **The code of governance the organisation has adopted**, e.g. the *Governance Code for Community, Voluntary and Charitable Organisations*, or the *Code of Practice for State Bodies*, etc.
- **Board members**, e.g. how they are selected in relation to diversity, skills and professional expertise; how many are non-executive; discussion of any induction for new board appointees; description of any board annual review and evaluation of its performance; any remuneration for board members; description of any policy for reimbursement of incidental expenses and board members' attendance at meetings.
- **Board meetings**, e.g. the number of meetings held during the year; process of the meetings and execution of board role.
- **Subcommittees of the board**, with a description of the subcommittees and their roles and composition.
- **Finance subcommittee**, with a description of its role in setting finance strategy and its role in the monitoring of budgets, management accounts and financial outcomes, and its role in reporting to the board for approval.
- **Risk management**, with a discussion of the risk environment and identification of the major risks, identification of any board subcommittee involved in reviewing or monitoring risk, and reporting risk to the board.

---

[1] The annual report of Concern was considered in the drafting of these guidelines as Concern won the Leinster Society of Chartered Accountants Ireland Published Accounts Award, Not-for-Profit Category in 2011 and 2012. The annual report of Arts Council England and its governance statement was also considered as a large and diverse arts organisation with many stakeholders.

For arts organisations, the risk of breaches of intellectual property and copyright, and the respect for artists' work is a special risk.
- **Internal control**, with a description of any review of effectiveness of internal control and assessment of the effectiveness of internal control, and any significant internal control issues.
- **Statement of compliance** with the *Corporate Governance Code* and departures from the Code (in accordance with the 'comply or explain' principle and stating which code is being followed).

Appendix 7

Suggested Guidelines for a Corporate Governance Review and Assessment for Arts Organisations

The board is primarily responsible for governance, and the review should be focused on the board.

Planning and Preparation

- Determine scope of the assessment. Document which governance code the organisation follows and assess that the code is appropriate to the organisation. Assess them on the basis of that code.[1]
- Carefully document and agree the terms of reference (as much of the information exchanged will be sensitive or confidential) to ensure that all of the work is in line with expectations of the board of the organisation.
- Determine who will be the main users of the review and assessment.
- Determine how report or feedback will be delivered and the deadline dates.
- Determine questionnaires to be used and their appropriate focus.
- List interviewees and questionnaire respondents, based on relevance.
- Plan and schedule a time for the review.
- Set milestones.
- Set dates for interim review and feedback to the board representative.

---

[1] The *Governance Code for Community, Voluntary and Charitable Organisations* and the SWiFT Code and the *Code of Practice for State Bodies* all state that they are based on the *UK Code of Corporate Governance* (formerly 'the Combined Code').

Document Review

Obtain and review:

- a list of all board members and others who periodically attend board meetings in a professional capacity, e.g. managers from within the organisation or advisors;
- Memorandums and Articles of Association;
- board minutes for the last two years, including AGMs and EGMs (if applicable);
- subcommittee minutes (if available);
- strategy statement;
- mission statement;
- vision statement;
- annual reports and financial statements for the last three (or five) years;
- monthly or quarterly management accounts;
- new board member induction process and board members' handbook; and
- review and complaints log, any pending insurance claims, and legal liabilities, as an assessment of ethical practice and compliance with health and safety and good business practices.

Interviews

Using questionnaires, carry out interviews with:

- board members or a sample of members, including the chair and heads of subcommittees, including:
  - at least one board member who is an artistic expert,
  - at least one board member who is an accountant, and
  - at least one board member who is a lawyer;
- the CEO and at least one member of the management team.

Conclusions and Recommendations

The objective of this assessment is to carry out a governance review for the purpose of making recommendations to improve corporate governance within the arts organisation. The review is not designed to compare or to 'rank' organisations. Therefore, the conclusions should form the basis for a report of governance programme items which were operating satisfactorily as well as 'governance gaps' (i.e. where governance can be improved). These can be presented with recommended actions to improve the governance standards being applied in the organisation.

Appendix 8

Document Review of Selected Grant Givers in the Irish Arts Sector

Funding Criteria	Arts Council					Ireland Funds	Dublin City Council	Dublin City Council
							Revenue	Project
	All	All	RFOs	RFOs	RFOs			
Grant Amount in euro	>650	>10k	<25k	>25k	>250k	<25k	<40k	<10k
ROI tax number	X	X	X	X	X		X	X
Tax clearance cert/ CHY		X	X	X	X		X	X
Bank account	X	X	X	X	X	X	X	X
Memo and articles	X	X	X	X	X	X		
Board meetings every 6 months			X	X	X			
Board meetings frequency							X	X
AC can attend board meetings?				X	X			
AC to receive board papers					X			
Income & exp./ financial returns		X					X	X
Audited accounts T/O >150k	X	X	X	X	X	X	X	
Certified grant expenditure					X			
Progress reports required?						X		
Is project sustainable?						X	X	X
Host project visits by funder	A system of peer review is in operation					X	A system of peer review is in operation	
50%–30% matching funds							X	X
Finance and governance details							X	X

Sources: The Arts Council, Conditions of Financial Assistance from the Arts Council
   The Ireland Funds, Application Guidelines Grant Round 2011
   The Ireland Funds Application Form
   Dublin City Council Arts Grant Application Form for 2012

Abbreviations: RFO – Regularly Funded Organisation

Appendix 9

Arts Council Income and Expenditure Report[1]

Grant Title:	
Company/Artist's name:	
Year:	

Income	€
Arts Council*	
Box Office Income	
Local Authority	
Guarantees	
Programme Sales	
Sponsorship	
Donations	
Other	
Total Income	
Expenditure	€
Salaries & Fees	
Technical & Production Costs	
Promotion & Publicity	
Administration	
Travel	
Accommodation	
Other	
Total Expenditure	
Surplus / (Deficit)	

[1] Source: courtesy of the Arts Council as at 2012.

Signature of Applicant:[1] _____

Signature of Auditor/Qualified Acountant:[2] _____

[1] Applicant is the individual who makes the application or in the case of a company or an organisation with a constitution other than that of a company an authorised signatory.

[2] Please refer to our terms and conditions to see when the additional signature of an auditor/ qualified accountant is required.

* Income from the Arts Council should be shown separately above. The full amount of the grant awarded must be shown. This can be split between amounts already received and amounts still outstanding.

Appendix 10

Comparison of Theoretical Perspectives on Organisational Governance[1]

Theory	Interests	Board members	Role of board	Model
Agency theory	Owners and managers have different interests	Owners' representatives	Compliance/ conformance: safeguard owners' interests; oversee management; check compliance	Compliance model
Stewardship theory	Owners and managers share interests	Experts	Improve performance: add value to top decisions/strategy partner/support management	Partnership model
Democratic perspective theory	Members/the public have different interests	Lay representatives	Political: represent constituents/ members; resolve conflicts; make policy; control executive	Democratic model
Stakeholder theory	Stakeholders have different interests	Stakeholder representatives: elected or appointed by stakeholder groups	Balance stakeholder needs: make policy/ strategise; control management	Stakeholder model
Resource dependency theory	Stakeholders and the organisation have different interests	Chosen for influence with key stakeholders	Boundary-spanning: secure resources; maintain stakeholder relations	Co-option model
Managerial hegemony theory	Owners and managers have different interests	Owners' representatives	Largely symbolic: ratify decisions; give legitimacy; managers have real power	'Rubber stamp' model

[1] Source: Cornforth, C., *The Governance of Public and Non-profit Organizations* (Routledge 2005), quoted in Turbide, J., "Can Good Governance Prevent Financial Crises in Arts Organizations?" (2012) Vol. 14, No. 2, *International Journal of Arts Management*, 4–16.

Appendix 11

Analysis of Arts Council Awards 2011–2012[1]

Arts Council Awards Analysed:
Awards to Individuals and to Organisations

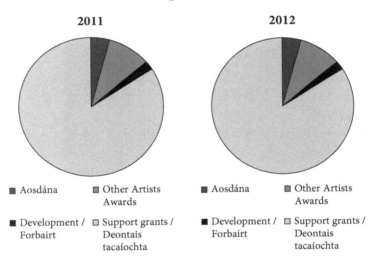

Arts Council Awards 2011 and 2012	2012	2011
Awards to individuals:	€	€
Aosdána	2,662,485	2,660,797
Other Artists Awards	7,561,985	6,962,772
Subtotals	10,224,470	9,623,569
Awards to organisations		
Development/Forbairt	907,360	958,202
Support grants/Deontais tacaíochta	45,420,153	47,426,561
Subtotals	46,327,513	48,384,763
Total awards	56,551,983	58,008,332
Percentage of total which is awarded to organisations	82%	83%

[1] Source: the Arts Council Financial Statements for the year ended 2012 and 2011, (http://www.artscouncil.ie/Publications/Arts_Council_Annual_Report_2010.pdfartscouncil.ie/en, accessed June 2013).

Results explained

The pie charts and table above show that most of the awards granted by the Arts Council are to organisations rather than to individuals.

Implications of the Results

Since 82% of Arts Council awards were granted to organisations rather than individuals in 2012, corporate governance is therefore relevant for 82% of Arts Council funding.

Useful Resources, Selected Organisations and Information Sources

Association of Compliance Officers in Ireland (ACOI)

The ACOI's purpose is to promote, for the public benefit, the advancement and dissemination of knowledge, information, views and ideas in the field of regulatory compliance and business ethics. See www.acoi.ie.

Arts Council of Ireland

See www.artscouncil.ie.

Arts Council England

Arts Council England is the national development agency for the arts in England. See www.artscouncil.org.uk.

Boardmatch Ireland

See www.boardmatch.ie.

Boardmatch Ireland supports the development of the community and voluntary sector (i.e. the not-for-profit sector) by strengthening boards and management committees.

Boardsource

Boardsource is a US organisation whose slogan is "Building Effective Nonprofit Boards". See www.boardsource.org.

Carmichael Centre

The largest shared services facility for voluntary and community organisations in Ireland. See www.carmichaelcentre.ie.

Carver Governance

Provides a theoretical foundation for the board's governance role in business, non-profit (NGO) and government organisations. See www.carvergovernance.com.

Chartered Accountants Ireland

See www.charteredaccountants.ie.

Chartered Accountants Ireland is a membership body of 23,000 members across the globe. Its role is to educate, represent and support its members.

Deloitte

Deloitte's useful corporate governance website is at www.corpgov.deloitte.com.

Companies Registration Office

The Companies Registration Office is the central repository of public statutory information on Irish companies and business names. See www.cro.ie.

Corporate Governance Association of Ireland

See www.cgai.ie.

The Corporate Governance Association of Ireland is an independent association which seeks to promote high standards of corporate governance by adhering to the association's Code of Professional Conduct.

National Council for Voluntary Organisations (NCVO)

The largest umbrella body for the voluntary and community sector in England. See www.ncvo-vol.org.uk.

Office of the Director of Corporate Enforcement

The Director of Corporate Enforcement encourages compliance with the requirements of the Companies Acts. See www.odce.ie.

University College Dublin Michael Smurfit Graduate Business School

To meet the growing educational needs of company directors, the UCD Centre for Corporate Governance was established in 2002. The centre runs the Director Development Programme, which consists of courses for Irish company directors covering all aspects of corporate governance. See www.ucd.ie/corpgov.

The Wheel

A support and representative body connecting community and voluntary organisations and charities across Ireland. Established in 1999, it has evolved to become a resource centre and forum for the community and voluntary sector. See www.thewheel.ie.

ERB

This website is a collaborative initiative between the Carmichael Centre, the Wheel and the CSEF (Community Sector Employers' Forum), providing employer resources for non-profits. See www.erb.ie.

The Global Corporate Governance Forum

This is an international finance corporation (IFC) multi-donor trust fund facility located within IFC Advisory Services. The Forum was co-founded by the World Bank and the Organisation for Economic Co-operation and Development (OECD) in 1999. Through its activities, the forum aims to promote the private sector as an engine of growth, reduce the vulnerability of developing and transition economies to financial crisis, and provide incentives for corporations to invest and perform efficiently in a socially responsible manner. See www.gcgf.org.

Bibliography

Accounting Standards Board, "Financial Reporting Standard for Public Benefit Entities and Consequential Amendments to Proposals in FRED 44 Financial Reporting Standard for Small and Medium-sized Entities", Exposure Draft, Number 45 (London 2011).

Arts Council England, "Endowments in the Arts, Commissioned by the Secretary of State for Culture, Olympics, Media and Sport" (2010).

The Arts Council of Ireland, *A Practical Guide for Board Members of Arts Organisations* (2006).

The Arts Council of Ireland, *Assessment of Economic Impact of the Arts in Ireland* (November 2009) by Indecon International Economic Consultants.

The Arts Council of Ireland, *Assessment of the Economic Impact of the Arts in Ireland* (November 2011) Arts and Culture Scoping Research Project by Indecon International Economic Consultants.

The Arts Council of Ireland, *Assessment of Economic Impact of the Arts in Ireland: An Update Report* (November 2012) Arts and Culture Scoping Research Project by Indecon International Economic Consultants.

The Arts Council of Ireland, *Developing the Arts in Ireland: Arts Council Strategic Overview 2011–2013* (2011).

Atlantic Philanthropies website, www.atlanticphilanthropies.org/region/republic-ireland (accessed 5 July 2011).

Barker, P., "Ethics Fatigue – Regulation vs Integrity", *Accountancy Ireland,* October 2006.

Business to Arts, "Private Investment in Arts and Culture: Survey Report" (2008) by Deloitte.

Business to Arts, "Shining the light on successful sponsorship" (2010) by PricewaterhouseCoopers.

Chartered Accountants Ireland, *Accounting Standards and Guidance: Corporate Governance, The Combined Code on Corporate Governance* (Chartered Accountants Ireland, July 2003).

Credit Suisse, "Gender Diversity and Corporate Performance" (2012).

The Corporate Governance Association of Ireland, "The Irish Development NGOs Code of Corporate Governance" (2008) developed in Partnership with Dóchas.

Business to Arts, *Private Investment in Arts and Culture: Survey Report* (2008) by Deloitte.

Department of Arts, Heritage and the Gaeltacht, "Statement of Strategy 2011–2014" (2011).

Department of Foreign Affairs, "The Global Irish Economic Forum One Year On. A report on the follow up to the Global Irish Economic Forum at Farmleigh" (2010).

The Charity Commission, "Charities SORP (FRS 102): Accounting and Reporting by Charities: Statement of Recommended Practice applicable to charities preparing their accounts in accordance with the Financial Reporting Standard applicable in the UK and Republic of Ireland (FRS 102) (effective 1 January 2015)" (2014). The Charity Commission and Office of the Scottish Charity Regulator.

Deloitte Development LLC, "Hot Topics – Improving board effectiveness: Oversight of strategy" (2012).

Department of Community, Equality and Gaeltacht Affairs, "Principal features of the Charities Act 2009", www.pobail.ie/en/CharitiesRegulation (accessed 24 July 2011).

Department of Finance, *Code of Practice for the Governance of State Bodies* (2009).

Dóchas, "A Dóchas Briefing Charities Regulation & Legislation" (March 2006).

Donlon, P., "Governance in Arts Organisations in Ireland" in *Practitioner Perspectives on Nonprofit Governance* (Centre for Nonprofit Management, School of Business, Trinity College Dublin, 2005).

Donoghue, F., Prizeman, G., O'Regan, A. and Noël, V., *The Hidden Landscape: First Forays into Mapping Nonprofit Organisations in Ireland* (Centre for Nonprofit Management, School of Business, Trinity College Dublin, 2006).

Donoghue, F., O'Regan, A., McGee, S. and Donovan, A.M., "Exploring the Irish Fundraising Landscape: A report on the practice and scale of charitable fundraising from the Republic of Ireland" (Irish Charities Tax Research Limited, Centre for Nonprofit Management, School of Business, Trinity College Dublin, 2007).

Dublin City Council, "Dublin City Council Financial Regulations" (2007).

Duffy, D. and McCarthy, J., *The Management of Management: A Practical Guide to Corporate Governance* (Prospectus, 2004).

Dunn, P., "Strategic Responses by a Nonprofit when a Donor becomes Tainted" (2010) Vol. 39, No. 1, *Nonprofit and Voluntary Sector Quarterly*, 102–23.

Ebrahim, A., "The Many Faces of Nonprofit Accountability (Working Paper No. 10-069)" (Harvard Business School, 2010).

The Erfurt Meetings (No. 1), "Enhancing stakeholder diversity in the Board room" (March 2008) European Citizens' Seminars, Erfurt, Germany.

Eisner, E., *The Arts and the Creation of Mind* (Yale University Press, 2002).

European Commission, "Women in economic decision-making in the EU: Progress report: A Europe 2020 initiative" (2012).

European Commission, *The EU Corporate Governance Framework*, Green Paper (2011).

European Commission, "Study on monitoring and enforcement practices in corporate governance in the member states", Contract No. ETD/2008/IM/F2/126 (2009).

Everitt, A., *The governance of culture: approaches to integrated cultural planning policies* (Council of Europe, 1999).

Financial Reporting Council, *The UK Corporate Governance Code* (2010).

Financial Reporting Council, *The UK Stewardship Code* (2012).

Financial Reporting Council, *Guidance on Audit Committees* (2012).

Freeman R., Harrison J., Wicks A., Parmar B. and DeColle S., *Stakeholder Theory: The State of the Art* (Cambridge University Press, 2010).

Governance Code for Community, Voluntary and Charitable Organisations in Ireland (2011) www.governancecode.ie.

GuideStar, "Transparency Report. The State of Nonprofit Transparency: Voluntary disclosure practices" (2008).

Harrington, T., *Accounting and Reporting by Charities in the Republic of Ireland* (Chartered Accountants Ireland, 2011).

Higgs, D., "Review of the role and effectiveness of non-executive directors" (2003).

Hillman-Chartrand, H. and McCaughey, C., "The Arm's Length Principle and the Arts: An International Perspective – Past, Present and Future" in M.C. Cummings Jr. and J. Mark Davidson Schuster (eds.), *Who's to Pay For the Arts? The International Search for Models of Arts Support* (Americans for the Arts, 1989).

Holden, J., *Capturing Cultural Value: How culture has become a tool of government policy* (Demos, 2004).

Holland, K., "New Authority to Regulate Charities", *The Irish Times*, 10 July 2013.

Internal Revenue Service, "Tax Exempt Status for Your Organisation" Publication 557 (10/2010) www.irs.gov (accessed 7 July 2011).

International Finance Corporation, World Bank Group, "Stakeholder Engagement and the Board: Integrating Best Governance Practices" (Global Corporate Governance Forum, Focus 8, 2009).

International Financial Reporting Standards Foundation, "IFRS for SMEs Update" (2013).

Institute of Chartered Accountants in England and Wales, "Report of the Committee on the Financial Aspects of Corporate governance: The Code of Best practice" (1992).

The Ireland Funds, "Fostering Fundraising in Ireland" (2002).

Irish Charities Tax Research Ltd, "Statement of Guiding Principles for Fundraising" (2008).

Irish Nonprofits Knowledge Exchange, "Irish Nonprofits: What do we know?" (January 2012).

Irish Nonprofits Knowledge Exchange, "Sector briefing, 26th February 2010" www.irishnonprofits.ie (accessed 20 June 2011).

Janis, I.L., *Groupthink: Psychological Studies of Policy Decisions and Fiascoes* (Wadsworth, 2nd edition, 1982).

Joyner, B. and Payne, D., "Evolution and Implementation: A Study of Values, Business Ethics and Corporate Social Responsibility" (2002) Vol. 41, *Journal of Business Ethics*, 297–311.

Kaiser, M., *Leading Roles: 50 Questions Every Arts Board Should Ask* (Brandeis University Press, 2010).

Keane, M. and Zhang, W., "Cultural creative industries or creative (cultural) industries?" in Hu, Huilin (Eds.), *China's Cultural Industries Forum* (Shanghai People's Publishing, 2008).

Keynes, J.M., "National Self-Sufficiency" (1933) Vol. 22, No. 4, *The Yale Review*, 755–69.

Killian, S., *Corporate Social responsibility: A Guide with Irish Experiences* (Chartered Accountants Ireland, 2012).

Kirk, R., *A Practical Guide to New UK and Irish GAAP* (Chartered Accountants Ireland, 2014).

KPMG LLP, Glover S. and Prawitt, D.F., "Enhancing Board Oversight: Avoiding Judgment Traps and Biases" (Committee of Sponsoring Organisations of the Treadway Commission, 2012).

McAuliffe, J., "The Siren Alps", *The Value of the Arts* (The Arts Council, 2007).

McGee, S. and Donoghue, F., "The Conundrum of Fundraising in Nonprofit Organisations: A Story from Ireland" (2009) Vol. 21, Issue 4, *Journal of Nonprofit & Public Sector Marketing*, 367–83.

Mitchell, R., Agle, B. and Wood, D., "Toward a Theory of Stakeholder Identification and Salience: Defining the Principle of Who and What Really Counts" (1997) Vol. 22, No 4, *Academy of Management Review*, 853–86.

Moggridge, D.E., "Keynes, the Arts, and the State" (2005) Vol. 37, Issue 3, *History of Political Economy*, 535–55.

National Chamber Choir website, www.nationalchamberchoir.com (accessed 26 June 2011).

National Standards Authority of Ireland, *Code of Practice for Corporate Governance Assessment in Ireland* (2010) NSAI Standards, SWiFT 3000.

O'Farrell, I., *Values – Not Just for the Office Wall Plaque: How Personal and Company Values Intersect* (Evolution Consulting, 2012).

Office of the Director of Corporate Enforcement website, www.odce.ie (accessed 24 May 2011).

O'Kelly, E., *The Case for Elitism* (The Arts Council, 2007).

Organisation for Economic Co-operation and Development, *Principles of Corporate Governance* (OECD Publications Service, 2004).

Ottenhoff, B. and Ulrich, G., "More Money for Good" (GuideStar, 2012).

Pope, N., "A Boardroom Guide to Organisational Capacity Building: Overcoming the Management Deficit in Ireland's Not-For-Profit Sector" (2012) (2into3.com, accessed 4 November 2012).

Certification Europe, "SWiFT 3000: 2010 Code of Practice for Corporate Governance Assessment" (http://certificationeurope.com/certification/swift-3000-corporate-governance-assessment, accessed October 2014.)

Quinlan, P. and Millar, E., "Companies Bill 2012" (2013) Vol. 45, No. 1, *Accountancy Ireland*.

Roche, B., "Garda enquiry at Cork Opera House", *The Irish Times*, 17 August 2010.

Radbourne, J., "Performing on Boards: The link between Governance and Corporate Reputation in Nonprofit Arts Boards" (2003) Vol. 6, No. 3, *Corporate Reputation Review*, 212–22.

Robinson, A. and Wasserman, N., *The Board Member's Easier Than You Think Guide to Nonprofit Finances* (Emerson & Church, 2012).

Sealy, R., Doldor, E., Singh, V. and Vinnicombe, S., *Women on Boards: 6 months Monitoring Report, October 2011* (Cranfield University School of Management, 2011).

Senge, P., Kleiner, R., Roberts, C., Roth, G., Ross, R. and Smith, B., *The Dance of Change* (Doubleday, 1999).

Shatter, A., "Minister for Justice and Equality, Alan Shatter's speech at the ICTR Annual Conference: Thursday, 10 November 2011", www.justice.ie (accessed 22 August 2012).

Sheehan, M., "Five community groups lost State funding last year: Money held back over 'major concerns'", *Irish Independent*, 2 January 2011.

Throsby, D., *Economics and Culture* (Cambridge University Press, 2001).

Tipton, G., "The artists who stay out in the cold", *The Irish Times*, 1 February 2013.

Turbide, J., "Can Good Governance Prevent Financial Crises in Arts Organizations?" (2012) Vol. 14, No. 2, *International Journal of Arts Management*, 4–16.

Turbide, J., Laurin, C., Lapierre, L., Morissette, R., "Financial Crisis in the Arts Sector: Is Governance the Illness or the Cure?" (2008) Vol. 10, No. 2, *International Journal of Arts Management*, 4–13.

Upchurch, A.R., "John Maynard Keynes, the Bloomsbury Group and the Origins of the Arts Council Movement" (2004) Vol. 10, No. 2, *International Journal of Cultural Policy*, 203–17.

Upchurch, A.R., "Keynes's Legacy: An Intellectual's Influence Reflected in Arts Policy" (2011) Vol. 17, No. 1, *International Journal of Cultural Policy*, 69–80.

Velasquez, M.G., *Business Ethics: Concepts and Cases* (Pearson, 7th edition, 2014).

The Wheel, *Solid Foundations* (2007).

The Wheel, *Getting to Grips with Governance* (2008).

Williamson, O., "Corporate Governance" (1984) Vol. 93, No. 7, *Yale Law Journal*, 1197–1230.

Index